Mine's Parkinson's, What's Yours?

A Story of Hope and Encouragement as
You Walk Life's Struggles and Hardships

Charles E. Mickles, Jr.

Copyright © 2020 Charles E. Mickles, Jr.

All rights reserved.

ISBN: 9798653179495

DEDICATION

I WOULD LIKE TO DEDICATE THIS WORK TO MY AMAZING AND BEAUTIFUL WIFE.

SHE HAS WALKED WITH ME THROUGH CONSTANT HEALTH STRUGGLES AND CHALLENGES, AND EVEN IN THE FACE OF THIS LATEST, LIFE-CHANGING DIAGNOSIS, CONTINUES TO AMAZE ME WITH HER LOVE, CARE, AND STRENGTH. SHE IS A TESTIMONY TO ME OF COURAGE AND DETERMINATION, AND SHE IS WHY I CONTINUE TO FIGHT.

I WILL LOVE YOU ALWAYS WITH ALL OF MY HEART, BABE. THANK YOU FOR LOVING, SUPPORTING, AND CARING FOR ME, AND ENCOURAGING ME TO COMPLETE THIS STORY.

Table of Contents
Mine's Parkinson's, What's Yours?

Introduction
A Parkinson's Prayer   1

Our Journey Begins   3
    1. *Four Little Words*   4
    2. *Am I Going Crazy?*   7
    3. *When Is Enough, Enough?*   10
    4. *Can You Trust Me?*   13
    5. *Being Okay with Not Being Okay*   15

Dark Days   18
    6. *I Am So Tired of The Fight*   19
    7. *Fear of The Future*   22
    8. *A Life Sentence*   25
    9. *When All Hope Seems Lost*   27
    10. *It Is Not Well With My Soul*   30

My Focus   33
    11. *My Focus Determines My Reality*   34
    12. *A Heaven of Hell, Or A Hell of Heaven*   37
    13. *Sleepless Nights*   41
    14. *Some Days I Feel Like Frodo Baggins*   44
    15. *What's Really Important*   46
    16. *It Really Is A Wonderful Life*   49
    17. *Pain Is The Great Confuser*   52

Well, This Stinks   55
    18. *That Life Stinks Bucket Is Getting Pretty Full*   56
    19. *God, This Plan Really Stinks*   59
    20. *Planning For The Unthinkable*   62
    21. *Sad, Discouraged, and Depressed, But Still Trusting God*   64

Letting Go   67
    22. *Playing "That" Card*   68
    23. *The "Handicap" Placard*   71

24. No More Bus Driving For You 74
25. When Your Dreams Are Dying 77

Bright Spots in my Darkness 80
    26. Learning To Live In The Moment 81
    27. It's The Little Things 84
    28. Our Blind Spot 86

Learning to Laugh Again 89
    29. Picking My Theme Song, My
        Warped Sense of Humor 90
    30. My Support, My Warped Sense
        of Humor, Part 2 93

So Many Questions 95
    31. Can He Still Use Me? 96
    32. Am I Enough? 99
    33. God, I Just Don't Get It 103
    34. How Will My Suffering Be Used? 106
    35. Where are you God? (When God Is Silent) 110

Emotional Ups & Downs 113
    36. Some Tears Are Needed 114
    37. Can I Forgive Myself: Battling Guilt 117
    38. A Terrifying Prospect 120
    39. So Alone 125
    40. Put On A Happy Face – How Can
        I Be Positive? 128

Walking The Journey With Us 131
    41. Buckle Up For The Roller Coaster Ride 132
    42. Drifting Apart 135
    43. We All Need A Sam 138
    44. My Online Community 141
    45. Silence Can Be Golden 144
    46. What's Wrong With You 147
    47. In Sickness And In Health 150

What I Am Learning 153
    48. …But God – There Is Always Hope 154

49. As Elvis Would Say, "I'm All Shook Up"	157
50. It Is Better With My Soul	160
51. Some Days I Just Need To Count My Blessings	163
52. I Am Not Thankful For Parkinson's	166
53. It's You I Like	169
54. He Is Good No Matter What	172

Life On This Journey	175
55. 10 Things I Wish People Understood About Living With Parkinson's	176
56. 10 More Things I Wish People Understood About Living With Parkinson's	179
57. Things Only A Caregiver Understands	182
58. What's It Like For Kids Walking This Path?	187
59. How Does This Affect Families?	190
60. Reflections: What a Difference A Year Makes	193

The Five (Most Important Lessons)	196
A Final Thought: Even When…	199
What Readers Are Saying	202
Acknowledgements	204
References/Sources	206
Author Biography	212

INTRODUCTION

SOME THINGS IN LIFE, YOU NEVER PLAN FOR, AND HONESTLY, NEVER EXPECT TO HAPPEN. DAY AFTER DAY PASSES WITHOUT INCIDENT, UNTIL, "WHACK," YOU ARE KNOCKED DOWN AND HAVE NO IDEA WHAT JUST HAPPENED. AS YOU LOOK AROUND TO SURVEY THE DAMAGE, YOU ARE NOT EVEN SURE WHAT TO DO NEXT. THAT IS HOW IT FELT LEARNING THAT I HAD PARKINSON'S AT THE AGE OF 44. NOTHING PREPARED US FOR THIS. WE REALIZED THIS JOURNEY WOULD BE UNLIKE ANY PATH WE HAD ALREADY WALKED.

GETTING THIS NEWS, ON TOP OF ALL THE OTHER ISSUES THAT I HAVE PHYSICALLY, WAS LIFE-CHANGING. IT IS CERTAINLY NOT ANYTHING THAT MY FAMILY OR I EVER EXPECTED, ESPECIALLY AT SUCH A YOUNG AGE. SO MANY QUESTIONS, SO MUCH UNCERTAINTY – MANY DAYS LEFT US ASKING, "WHERE ARE YOU GOD? WHY ME? WHY US?"

THIS IS A JOURNEY THAT I NEVER WANTED TO TAKE, BUT ONE THAT HAS BEEN THRUST UPON ME. AS I WALK THIS PATH, GOD IS ALREADY SHOWING ME MANY THINGS WHICH I HOPE TO SHARE WITH YOU. THIS IS NOT GOING TO BE SOME ROSE-COLORED PICTURE – THERE WILL BE LAUGHTER, AND THERE WILL BE TEARS; THERE WILL BE UPS, AND THERE WILL BE DOWNS. THERE WILL BE EXAMPLES OF FAITH AND FEAR – IT WILL BE A REALISTIC PICTURE OF WHAT GOD IS WALKING ME THROUGH PERSONALLY AND US AS A FAMILY. I INVITE YOU TO TAKE THIS JOURNEY WITH ME, AND I HOPE THAT THROUGH THIS, GOD SPEAKS TO YOUR HEART AND SHOWS YOU SOME OF THE SAME THINGS THAT HE IS REVEALING TO ME AS YOU WALK THE PATH HE HAS LAID OUT FOR YOU. THANK YOU FOR JOINING ME ON THIS JOURNEY, AS DAY BY DAY, WE FACE THE CHALLENGE OF LIVING WITH PARKINSON'S DISEASE. WE ALL HAVE CHALLENGES. MINE'S PARKINSON'S, WHAT'S YOURS?

Charles E. Mickles Jr.

A Prayer of a Parkinson's Patient

Most nights sleep eludes me, I rarely find rest.
I stumble and fall and my walking's not the best.
I'm stiff and I'm slow, and it's hard to get around
I laugh and I cry, and sometimes I'm down.

Often I wonder if I'll get through the week.
The road seems so long and the future looks bleak.
I many times wonder how I will fare,
And if I stopped in this place, I would be in despair.

I work to keep going with all of my might,
But my life and my day is more than this fight.
Daily this disease does greatly affect me,
But I will not let this illness define me.

I know you will give me the strength for each day,
And help as I walk on this difficult way.
I will not despair, or give into fear,
For you're always with me, so close and so near.

So today I simply ask for the strength to keep going,
To take the next step, and never quit fighting.
You have surrounded me with great love and support,
To walk with me, encourage me and always exhort.

Help me see the blessings I'm given each day,
To encourage and strengthen as I walk on this way.
Daily remind me why I continue to fight,
And help me see that my future's still bright.

Mine's Parkinson's, What's Yours?

In spite of the darkness, and in the blackest of night,
You will not abandon me in this tough fight.
You will always be here, walking with me,
In your rest and your peace, may I always be.

So today I say thank you for all that I see,
The ups and the downs, and each victory.
Thank you for those with me each step of the way,
And thank you for giving me one more sweet day.

Charles E. Mickles Jr.

Our Journey Begins

"For I know the plans I have for you", declares the LORD, "plans to prosper you and not harm you, plans to give you hope and a future." – Jeremiah 29:11

CHAPTER 1
FOUR LITTLE WORDS

"You have Parkinson's Disease." I sat there and stared at the doctor. Did I really hear what I thought I heard? My wife and I had gone into this appointment, expecting to hear something like this, but listening to the doctor say that was very sobering. There was almost a finality to it. Instantly, a thousand questions begin to pour through my mind. It felt overwhelming, and I honestly was not sure where to start. From this moment, life would never be the same.

It was like receiving a sucker punch in the gut. Nothing could have prepared me for that short, simple sentence. I did not even know where to begin, what to think, or what to ask. Thankfully my wife was there, and she was able to ask a few questions as I sat there trying to take it all in.

As we left that office, we realized that there was so much we did not know and that we were embarking on a journey that would carry us for the rest of our lives. So many questions, so many things to consider, so much uncertainty. To be honest, I could not even find my voice, and all the worst-case scenarios started pouring through my mind. Many family members and friends knew we had this appointment, and were waiting to hear, but I just couldn't talk, I just couldn't say it, for if I said it, then it became real.

Thankfully my wife was able to talk with others and share the news. (She is our planner, and her mind was already spinning with how we were going to fight this thing.) As we drove home, I sat there in stunned, complete silence – how could this be possible – I am only 44 years old for crying out loud? Surely there has been a mistake? God, haven't I already had enough health issues? How is my family going to survive this? On and on the questions went, as I sat there, fighting tears that just would not stop.

Every time I tried to speak, my voice cracked and failed me, my eyes would fill with tears, and despair would seek to overtake my spirit. After trying, again and again to choke out even a few words, I just gave up. Tired of crying, tired of choking up, and just plain tired, I closed my eyes and thought, what do we do next?

It was at this moment, God brought back to remembrance a verse that He gave me, almost exactly five years ago, when I was facing my third hip replacement. "I would have despaired unless I had believed that I would see the goodness of the Lord in the land of living. Wait for the Lord; be strong, and let your heart take courage; yes, wait for the Lord." (Psalm 27:13-14)

I sat there looking at my wife, and my heart broke for her. She did not deserve this life sentence, and this was not what she had signed up for, yet I knew that she loved me and that she would walk this path with me, no matter what the outcome. God, how are we going to make it? Staring at her and thinking of this verse, I was reminded that I was not alone. Not only did I have my faith, I had a remarkable life partner, and a family that would be walking with me into the abyss of Parkinson's.

There would be ups and downs. There would be days of faith, and there would be days we were drowning in doubt. There would be days of great sorrow, but there would also be days of laughter and days that would still be bright. No matter what, though, I would not walk this path alone, and together, we would face whatever came our way.

In that one moment, I was reminded that I have hope, for He is with me. As hard as it was to see and believe this at that moment, in my head and heart, I knew it to be true. He knows the path I'm beginning upon. He knows the end. He knows the ups and the downs we will have. He knows the faith and the doubts that will plague us. And most importantly, He knows how He will provide.

Each day we would choose how we faced this latest challenge. The future was frightening, but somehow, we would get through it. It would be hard, but together we would face it, and together we would walk forward, and He would give us the strength we needed each day.

This realization did not mean my sorrows were magically taken away. I was not jumping for joy at the prospect of yet another health struggle that would carry me through the rest of my life. This realization did not mean I was still not struggling with doubts, or that all my questions and fears were answered. I was simply reminded that in the face of devastating news, and an uncertain future, I could have hope. I could have faith that He is with me, and He will never leave me or forsake me.

As I stepped out onto this journey that no one ever wants to take, I knew there was somebody that was, and always will be, walking right beside me, and because of this, I can have hope.

CHAPTER 2
AM I GOING CRAZY?

For months, actually years, I had watched my body, bit by bit, betray me. I could tell that something was not right. I just did not feel like myself. (Granted, if you know me, you know that I have never been quite right, but this was different.) In spite of my other physical issues, I began to notice changes; I was starting to have more and more difficulty doing even basic things.

I really started to notice the difference when my tremors became worse. I had been to two different neurologists, both of which told me I merely had essential tremors. It was nothing too serious, and not something to be worried about. In the year before this appointment, there had been a steady slide in my health.

I began to have difficulty gripping things and doing just about any task with my hands. Writing and typing became almost impossible, and I was left to dictate anything I needed to send out. I grew a goatee, because shaving became very difficult. Combing my hair, getting dressed, even brushing my teeth, took forever, and sometimes, I could not even do this. Humiliated, this 43-year-old man would have to ask his wife to help him get dressed. (This is not supposed to happen for years!)

I struggled with being motivated and focusing on the task at hand.

Many times, I was left searching for words, or for my train of thought altogether. Every time I would see the doctor, I was told the same things, "This is the essential tremors," or "You're too young for something like Parkinson's." Every conceivable blood test was done. If a part of the body could be scanned or imaged, it was. Each and every time, the doctor would call back and say, "Everything looks normal," and once again, we would have no answers. Disheartened, discouraged, and so tried, I really began to think I was just losing my mind.

As I sat in the office of my third neurologist, he looked at me and said, "Are you depressed? Have you ever been diagnosed with depression? That could be causing the problem." I sat there, stunned, and thought, "Really, that is all you've got – I'm depressed; OF COURSE I'M DEPRESSED! (I wanted to scream!) I've gone from doctor to doctor to doctor, and I still do not have any answers. I feel like crap. I can't do any of the things that a normal 43-year-old should be able to do. I get test after test done, and they keep showing nothing is wrong with me, yet I know that is not the case. Yes, I am depressed, BUT THAT'S NOT THE PROBLEM!"

I wanted to scream, and I became more and more discouraged. I thought, "Maybe I am just going crazy; maybe this is just all in my head; maybe there really is nothing wrong with me." No matter where we looked for over a year, there were no answers, only more questions.

I was exhausted, I saw no light or answers in my future, and I was just so tired of fighting. As a person of faith, I struggled even finding comfort and strength in that. It is easy to have faith when we have all the answers, but true faith and trust require belief, even when we do not understand and cannot see the answers, and at this point, I was not even sure I could rest in that.

As I prayed and sought the Lord during this time, I was reminded that I am not the first one to have these questions or struggles. David, Job, Elijah, Esther, and so many others in Scripture, struggled with the same thing. David cried out, "Oh my God, I cry by day, but You do not answer; and by night, but I have no rest." If David had stopped here, it would be very discouraging, but he remembered all of the times that God had been faithful and had shown His goodness even in difficulties.

As we approached this appointment (with a fourth neurologist), I went in with very little hope, expecting to hear the same thing I had heard over and over again. So many emotions swirled through me. I was so afraid that they would find something wrong, but at the same time, fearful that they would not. I was discouraged, because time after time, I had been to these professionals and heard, "Everything looks fine," even though I knew it was not. Above all, I was tired. I was so exhausted physically and mentally from fighting the unknown in my body, and I really did not know if I could go on.

As I sat there, waiting to see my new specialist, I sat there with very little hope. I wanted answers, but at the same time, I did not, because most likely, the answer would not be a good one. I knew Parkinson's (or something even worse) was probably waiting for me in that exam room, and if not, then maybe I was just crazy. Either way, as the doctor came back into the room, I knew I would not want to hear what he had to say.

Whether answers came or not, I had to trust that God would provide the strength and grace needed to walk forward. As I said before, it is easy to have faith when we have all the answers, but true faith and trust requires belief even when we do not understand and cannot see the answers.

When he said those four little words, everything changed. I had an answer, but it was an answer I did not want. I realized that even after I finally had the answer that I had Parkinson's, I still did not have all the answers. My future was as uncertain as it ever had been, and my choice was still the same – I could choose to walk in faith and hope, or I could choose fear. It was a choice I would have to make each moment on this new journey. Either decision would drastically affect my walk forward. I do not know what each day will bring, or the choice I will make in the future, but today, I choose hope. Just like Elijah, David, Esther, and so many others, He is with me, and that gives me hope.

CHAPTER 3
WHEN IS ENOUGH, ENOUGH

As we drove home from the doctor, one question kept repeating over and over in my mind, "God, when is enough, enough?" You see, in regards to my health, this was not my first rodeo. From the age of 15, there had been a seemingly endless parade of health issues and difficult circumstances.

I was diagnosed with Rheumatoid Arthritis when I was only 15. In 3 months, it destroyed my hip. By 17, I was rushed to the hospital because the medication ate a hole in my stomach. I had my first hip replacement at 19. As the Arthritis spread, more challenges presented themselves. Then at the ages of 34 and 39, I had my second and third hip replacements. (I know, it sounds like such fun. Who else, at age 40, can say they've had three hip replacements?)

It would be great if it stopped there. Still, in the two years leading up to this new diagnosis, I had dealt with kidney stones, numerous broken toes, a diagnosis of Osteopenia, the development of heart issues, sleep apnea, high blood pressure, and, oh, yes, the removal of some skin cancer. Move over Job, there is a new kid in town.

In addition to my health issues, our family had also dealt with numerous family tragedies. The loss of my sister to cancer was devastating, and three months later, my dad being diagnosed with cancer shook us to our core. My wife had very difficult pregnancies, being hospitalized numerous times, and also had her own health struggles. (I mean, I could not have all the fun.) Through sickness, miscarriages, financial uncertainty, and even death, our entire family pushed forward.

This list could go on and on, and needless to say, like many of us, we had many difficult times. It was to the point, where I was afraid to ask "what next" because I really didn't want to know. If bad things came in 3's, it must've been multiplied by 10, or else we were mixed up with another "Mickles' family." Many times, I double-checked just to make sure my name was not Job.

I was not looking for some great blessings. I was not asking for millions, or a huge mansion, or any of the "toys" that seem so important. I simply wanted a break. Couldn't I just have some normalcy in life? Boring sounded so appealing. Lord, just a year, a month, or even just a week with no excitement, no difficulty, and no tragedy. Sadly, that just did not seem to be in the cards.

As we drove home, I thought of all these things, and thought, "Really God, when is enough, enough? Look at all our family has walked through – isn't that enough? Don't we deserve a break?" I'm not really sure what I expected to hear. Maybe you've asked a similar question, or had comparable feelings. I'm not sure there's a right answer. We can look at our circumstances, things we have walked through, and feel like we've done our bit. "Okay, God, I've had my fill of struggles; now it's time to move on to someone else."

In reality, though, I was not really asking, "When is enough, enough?" Actually, I think my real question of God was, "How do I walk through this? How do I face something that, short of a miracle, will never end and will only get worse? How do I adjust to this 'New Normal?' How do I survive a battle that, in the end, I will lose?" I was overwhelmed. I honestly could not see how my family would make it.

My answer came a few days later. In Matthew 6:34, Jesus reminds us, "Do not be anxious about tomorrow." In II Corinthians 12:9, God tells Paul, "My grace is sufficient for you, for my power is made perfect in weakness." In that moment, reading those verses, God reminded me, that I only needed grace for today, for this hour, and for this moment. He showed me that as my body grew weaker, He would be my strength, and He would give me and my family the daily grace we needed to walk forward.

The real question was not, when is enough, enough, but instead, would I trust Him? With the uncertainty that my future held, would I trust Him? Would I rest in His grace and strength to see me through this latest struggle? Would I trust Him with the provision for my family? Would I trust Him with my future?

I realized that this was not a one-time choice, but one that I would have to make every day, every hour, and every moment. It was one that would shape not only my future but daily how I walked this path. The choice I face each moment is mine alone to make, and that choice will determine how I choose to walk through this. Would I trust Him? Yes, I will. Trusting Him will not always be simple, and many days it will not make sense. Trusting Him will mean I do not have all the answers, but that is okay, because He does, and it is a choice only I can make.

CHAPTER 4
CAN YOU TRUST ME?

In the days after my diagnosis, I will be honest, my head was spinning. It was like staring at an immense mountain, knowing you have to climb it, but having no idea where and how to start. So many questions; so much uncertainty; so much doubt; and yes, so much anger and pain.

As I sat there staring at this insurmountable mountain, it reminded me of the times in college when I had this enormous project to do, and just did not know where to begin. Parkinson's, though, was not just like a mountain, it was like a mountain going through an earthquake – circumstances and symptoms continually changing, and no two people's path up that mountain precisely the same.

We realized very quickly there might be hundreds of paths up this mountain of Parkinson's, with no guide to show us the way. You see, with this disease, there is a lot of uncertainty. Will this become debilitating in 2 years or 20? Will I be able to work 5 more years, 10, or 20? How long will I be mobile – will I need a wheelchair? Will I have to stop driving in a year or 10 years?

The more my wife and I researched and tried to plan, the more we realized we could not. With this latest health struggle, it again felt like the rug had been pulled out from under us. Just when we thought everything was settled, and we were finally getting into a good place, wham – this latest struggle hit us out of nowhere.

We all live with this illusion of control. We carefully plan, we make arrangements for the future, we order our lives and our days. We sit back and pretend that we have somehow mastered our own destiny. Yet this illness quickly brings to the forefront how little control we have and how uncertain our future truly is.

I wonder if this is how Joseph ever felt in Scripture? Every time he thought things were going in the right direction, the rug was pulled out from under him, and he was left asking the question, "What in the world just happened?" Yet even through that uncertainty, Genesis clearly points out numerous times, "and the Lord was with Joseph." Even the man who had visions and dreams of the future, did not know how God was going to work and when His plan would unfold.

In truth, the day I was diagnosed, my future was not any more or less uncertain than it had been 5 minutes before. Sure, it seemed that way, but whether I had this illness or not, I had no idea what the future would hold, but He did. He knows my path, He has numbered my days, and He knows how He will provide. Whether I have Parkinson's or not, I do not know my future, but He does.

As I considered all of these things, it was as if I could clearly hear God saying, "Do you trust me?" Even with all the uncertainty, through all of the pain, will you still trust me? This decision is not made once, but over the course of hours, days, and weeks. In the good times when I'm feeling great, or during the "off times" when I am struggling, will I trust Him?

I wish I could say that my answer has always been yes, but honestly, there are days of doubting, days when I struggle seeing Him in the midst of the pain and sorrow, days when it is hard. Can I trust Him? This is a question I must ask and answer each and every day, but the beautiful thing about my Lord, is no matter where I am, or if I am struggling, He is always with me, and because of that, I can trust Him.

CHAPTER 5
BEING OKAY WITH NOT BEING OKAY

The joy of the Lord should be my strength. I should be anxious for nothing. Trusting the Lord in all things should be my default response by this point in life. In everything, I should give thanks, and I should rejoice in the Lord always. All of these things I have heard and believed since my youth. Yet today, I am just not there. How can I be thankful and rejoice and not worry about this latest struggle? Some Christian I am turning out to be.

Walking the path of this latest diagnosis, I have realized that once again, I am struggling with these things. Sadly, this is not the first time I have felt this way. As I have had more health struggles, more challenges and difficulties, and more loss, I must admit that I have been frustrated with myself at how I respond. I would beat myself up for not responding as I thought a believer should.

Since childhood, I had heard passages such as:

"In everything give thanks." – I Thessalonians 5:18
"Rejoice in the Lord always; and again I say rejoice."
– Philippians 4:8
"The joy of the Lord is your strength." – Nehemiah 8:10

"Do not be anxious about anything..." – Philippians 4:6
"Trust in the Lord with all your heart..." – Proverbs 3:5

As I struggled through trial after trial, I heard these statements, not always as promises and encouragements, but sometimes as indictments. They highlighted where I was not. I felt none of these things, and instead of being encouraged, it was a reminder to me that I was not a "good little Christian." I was not responding how a Christian should, and in this latest difficulty, I was failing.

I would sit there and beat myself up for not responding to challenges as I was taught. As I beat myself up, I would get more and more discouraged, and pull away from the God and faith I so desperately needed as I walked through this challenge. I was defeated and felt like, as a believer, I was failing.

I spent years in this place, and honestly, sometimes I am still there. I see my responses and wonder why I am still struggling with these same things. God has been faithful and provided. He has walked with me and strengthened me through so much, why shouldn't I be rejoicing, thankful, and trusting? After years of beating myself up, I am beginning to see the answer – I am human.

I realize it is not only natural but reasonable to struggle in this way. I discovered that there are also passages that share these thoughts:

"...A time to weep...a time to mourn" – Ecclesiastes 3:4
"The Lord is close to the brokenhearted and saves those who are crushed in spirit." – Psalm 34:18
"He heals the brokenhearted..." – Psalm 147:3
"Blessed are those who mourn, for they shall be comforted." – Matthew 5:4
"...weep with those who weep." – Romans 12:15

As I read these passages, I realize something profound – it is okay, not to be okay. Even as a believer, we will have sorrow and doubt. We will struggle. We are not expected to skip through life like nothing is wrong spouting Biblical platitudes. God does not expect us to paste a smile on our face like nothing is wrong and deny the struggle and emotions we are feeling.

As believers, we will have the same emotions as every other person on the planet, and it does not make us less of a Christian just because we are struggling. We certainly should not beat ourselves up for our feelings and for fighting with things that any person would when faced with difficulties.

I also began to look back at the passages I first listed and realized something. In each situation, it is the Lord, not my circumstances. I should be rejoicing in the Lord, trusting in the Lord, and being thankful, not for the struggle, but for the Lord. You see, I can be sorrowful and still have His joy, strength, and peace.

Sometimes, those around us, whether Christian or not, do not know how to respond to tragedy. Instead of dealing with the emotions or sitting in the mud with someone, we try to encourage ourselves or others with verses, that while true, can sometimes feel hollow.

Yes, we need to be reminded of these promises and truths, but we also need to be reminded that sorrow and questions are okay. We need to be reminded that we will feel these things strongly, and that is okay. The difference is, we have hope, and our sorrow does not have to be the end. While we do not want to camp out there, grief and tears are good, and sometimes we need to weep with one another.

As we are weeping together, we need to remind each other that while we have all of these beautiful and true promises, it really is okay not to be okay.

Dark Days

"Even though I walk through the darkest valley, I will fear no evil, for you are with me; your rod and your staff, they comfort me." – Psalm 23:4

CHAPTER 6
I AM SO TIRED OF THE FIGHT

30 years. It's been 30 years since I first heard the words, you have arthritis. I was only 15 years old at the time, and I had no way of knowing just how long this journey would be, and at times, how challenging and exhausting it would be some days.

When you're 15, it is hard sometimes to understand the full scope of anything. Often you don't see much past today, and it's just sometimes hard to understand the seriousness of something. That was how it was when I was told I had arthritis. I realized there would be challenges, I understood that there would be difficulties, I assumed there would be pain. Still, I did not understand how exhausting the fight would be somedays.

For 30 years, day in and day out, I have fought my body. I do not remember what a day without pain feels like. On top of the arthritis, because of the medicines I have to take, and just getting older, more and more problems kept piling up. And now, on top of everything, I have Parkinson's – none of these diseases have a cure, we can only treat the symptoms and hope to slow down the progression. Not a real encouraging thought.

In the lead up to my diagnosis of Parkinson's, there were many days of unbearable pain and exhaustion. I could not do the most simple things, and anything I tried to do, took 10 times the effort. In pain, exhausted, and frustrated, there were so many times when I sat beside my wife with tears in my eyes and simply said, "I don't know how much longer I can do this; I am so tired of the fight."

In my head, I knew I would never get better. Yes, we might be able to ease the symptoms; yes, we may be able to slow down the disease, but healing, short of a miracle, would never happen. I knew each day would be a struggle, and the older I got, the harder the battle would become. Every day I would have to fight my body to do the things that most people took for granted. And now, on top of everything, I had one more diagnosis, one more challenge, one more difficulty – Parkinson's – to add to the pile.

I will be honest, when I heard this diagnosis, my first thought was, "I'm so tired of the fight. God, how can you give me one more thing to deal with? Haven't I fought enough – don't I have enough challenges already?" By this point, I was so tired (even struggling to find out what I had) that I didn't know if I could fight anymore.

I think if we all look at our lives, we can find areas where we would say, "I'm just so tired of the fight." Maybe it's finances, health, family issues – whatever the area is, many of us have been or are in this place. A place where we are ready to give up and throw in the towel, and simply say, "I'm done, I'm out of here."

We all have days or times in our lives like this. Days where we just do not think that we can take another step. Many days I have been in this place, days when I sat there in tears thinking, "How do I go on, how do I keep fighting – fighting a battle I know I will never win?"

It is in those moments that the Lord, and those around me, help me to refocus and remind me that HE will give me the strength to keep fighting.

Isaiah 40:29, 31 "He gives strength to the weary…the Lord will renew their strength…".
Psalm 46:1 "God is our refuge and strength…".

Nehemiah 8:10 "...the joy of the Lord is your strength."
Psalm 28:7 "The Lord is my strength and my shield...".
Psalm 118:14 "The Lord is my strength and my defense...".

On and on, in promise after promise, we are reminded that God will give us strength, day by day, to fight the battles set before us. In these conversations, my wife would also remind me I'm fighting for them – for my family – and with these reminders, one day at a time, I find the strength to keep fighting.

Am I tired of the fight? Absolutely. Do I have the strength to keep fighting? Day by day, most definitely, for I am fighting for myself and my family, and HE will give me the power I need to fight, one day at a time.

CHAPTER 7
FEAR OF THE FUTURE

As a young child of the 80's, Schoolhouse Rock told me "knowledge is power" and G.I. Joe taught me, "knowing is half the battle." Today, we have more knowledge than ever available to us at our finger tips – but is that knowledge really giving us power? Sometimes, that knowledge can make the battle even harder.

I grew up in a time before the Internet, before Google, and before smartphones – or as my children call it – the stone age. During that time, we had limited sources of information available to us. We could look at encyclopedias, newspapers, the evening news, but information was not always right at our fingertips. We could not simply type in a topic, and an endless stream of information appear before us.

Now, whenever we want it, information is right there. When we were still looking for a diagnosis, I would often get on Google or WebMD and type in my symptoms (not always a wise choice). The results I would find would amaze and frighten me at their scope. Everything between minor tremors to ALS would show up. Depending on my mood, it would give me some false hope, or scare the crap out of me.

When the doctor gave me the trial of Parkinson's medicine, and it started working, I began doing some research on these same platforms. I was able to find useful information about things I was currently dealing with, and many of my symptoms were explained. There was also a lot of "helpful" information on the progression of this disease.

Now don't get me wrong, it can be very good to know what to expect. It can help you plan and prepare for the future. There can also be a very real downside to this information – fear. For Parkinson's, the future can look pretty bleak. I read about all of these things that would happen or could happen, and it was very easy for my mind to go to the worst-case scenario. In fact, as the doctor shared with me my diagnosis, much of the information I had read began streaming through my mind.

I began to think about all the things that might happen, and what very well my future could look like. And in those moments, my heart was gripped with fear. Fear of the path that I was now on. Fear of what would happen to my body and mind. Concern for my family. Fear of what the future would look like. Fear of how we would plan and provide for the future. Even some doubt in myself and my ability to face this.

This can be the danger of knowledge without perspective. Knowledge in a vacuum, without perspective and context, can be a very overwhelming and frightening thing, and can sometimes give us the wrong picture, or lead us to incorrect conclusions. You see, in all of this knowledge that I was gathering, one thing was lacking – experience.

The only experience I had was what I had read, and the way I felt without any treatment. As I sought knowledge, I began to find individuals and groups who had or were walking the same path that I was starting out upon. They had the experience that I did not and helped give me the perspective that I did not yet have.

I began to realize that yes, knowledge is essential, but so is faith and perspective. Hebrews 11:1 reminds us, "Now faith is the assurance of things hoped for, the conviction of things not seen." Fear and faith both deal with the same thing – an unknown future. Both are based on what we cannot see. When presented with events, or even the knowledge of what might happen, I have two choices in my response: fear or faith.

I can respond in faith, trusting that God will walk me through these events. When I have knowledge of what might happen, I can choose to believe that God will give me the strength and provision I need. I can take that knowledge and begin to plan for the future, trusting God's direction. Or on the flip side, I can use that knowledge and become fearful of what might happen and of what the future might look like, living in fear and defeat.

Whether you have Parkinson's or not, or some other difficulty, you have the same choice. Before my diagnosis, I had the same decision. I can live in fear of the future and let the knowledge cripple me, or I can take that knowledge, and decide to trust that God will sustain me and strengthening me for the fight ahead.

This is not a one-time choice, but the decision that I choose to make each and every day, sometimes hour by hour. There are days when fear grips my heart and when I am fighting despair. There are days when it is easy to trust and live in faith. This is a very real struggle we all face, and there are many times when I'm starting down that road of fear, that I have to stop and turn to Him, or have others encourage me along the way. In those times, I must remember that I do not know what my future holds, but He does, and because He does, I can have faith.

CHAPTER 8
A LIFE SENTENCE

I hereby sentence you to life without the possibility of parole. This is how it felt. When I first heard the diagnosis of Parkinson's disease, I knew I was being given a life sentence. There would be no "parole," and the only chance of early release would be death. This new prison I found myself in would be with me the rest of my life, and it felt hopeless.

Being diagnosed with a chronic illness feels this way, yet this life sentence was not just for me but for my family also. I was dealing with the pain and the degeneration. They were dealing with all the other effects of this disease. It was adding additional burdens to them and challenges for our family.

Instead of being locked away in a cell, I was locked away in a body that was failing. I was locked away in a body that was slowly degenerating and getting worse. The life sentence my family was facing was, in many ways, more challenging.

They were watching someone they loved suffer and were helpless to stop it.
They were limited in what they could do by the limitations I had.
There were experiences they missed out on, because I could not do them.

They were limited financially because of the expense of my care. They were isolated because few were walking the same path.

They, like me, were serving a life sentence in a prison they could not change. Yet even in this prison, in the course and hopelessness of this life sentence, we have a cellmate that will never leave us. This cellmate would serve out the life sentence with us. Only this Cellmate could provide a reprieve, and change a life sentence into a life-changing experience. He could provide hope.

Psalm 30:11 tells us, "You have turned for me my mourning into dancing; You have loosed my sackcloth and clothed me with gladness." Nothing is exciting or joyous about a Parkinson's Diagnosis, or really any struggle. Being a Christian does not mean we skip through life oblivious to pain and sorrow. It does, though, mean that our pain and struggles are not the end of the story. It does not have to define us.

Throughout Scripture, we see promise after promise of Christ walking with us, of being our strength, of being our joy, and being our defense. He is with my family and me in this life sentence, and that gives us hope. Lamentations 3:22-23 reminds us, "The steadfast love of the Lord never ceases; his mercies never come to an end; they are new every morning, great is your faithfulness."

New every morning – that is His promise to us. Day by day is how we must walk through these struggles. Whatever path or life sentence you find yourself in, remember He is with you. Trust Him to be your hope and supply day by day.

CHAPTER 9
WHEN ALL HOPE SEEMS LOST

It was a dark day, darker than any day I had yet experienced. As I listened, on the other end of the phone, my mom said something that rocked me to my core, "Your father has advanced colon cancer." I had no words. So many emotions were pouring through me. "Please, God, not again, please do not do this to my family again," was all I could say as I struggled to process this latest news.

Only 3 months earlier, we had laid my sister to rest after she lost her battle with brain cancer. She had been diagnosed only 6 months before her passing at the age of 25. The disease had quickly progressed, and in just a few short months, she was gone. As we stood around her hospital bed saying goodbye, I did not think it could get any darker. So much pain, so much sorrow, so many questions – I was wrong; it was about to get darker still.

With emotions still raw from this loss, we had now been placed in another life-changing battle. I was at school when I got the news, and was given the task of telling my sister. When I found her and told her, we stood there on the sidewalk, holding each other, crying, having no idea what to do or where to turn. "God, how could you be doing this again? Not again, please God, not again," was all either of us could choke out between tears.

Fear, sorrow, hurt, anger, doubts, and pain were all choking out what little light we could still see. All the worse case scenarios poured through our minds. Very little hope seemed to exist as we approached his surgery, a surgery that could have dire consequences for my father and his family. When you add to that the constant health struggles I and my wife were facing at the time, and my father's looming job loss, it was very dark indeed.

I became numb and apathetic to so many things – my family, my ministry, my friends – as I slowly withdrew into myself. I felt utterly hopeless. I was hurt, and I was angry with God for doing this to us again. I found myself lashing out in pain at others, and very close to throwing away my family and ministry. I was done serving a God who would do this to us.

My dad's surgery went well, and he is now over 15 years cancer free (praise the Lord), but those months and years after were very hard for my family and me. In these struggles, I had lost all hope, and I was honestly just going through the motions. Thankfully, I had some friends, brothers really, who would not let me go. They walked with me through this and helped me see that God was still with me and that there was hope.

This summer, I found myself in much the same place. When the doctor spoke those four little words, my world was once again rocked. "Not again, God. Not another health issue. Don't I already have enough on my plate with ALL the health issues I already have? How can you do this to my family?" These and many other thoughts rolled through my head. I knew this was going to be the hardest fight I had faced yet, and it was one that most likely in the end, I would lose. How could I possibly find hope in the midst of this? I saw no way that this would be good.

As I considered these things, and talked through them (as I could) with others, God reminded me of a very simple verse. "Now, faith is the assurance of things HOPED for, and the conviction of things NOT SEEN (emphasis mine)." (Hebrews 11:1) Things hoped for…things not seen. In that one small verse, I was reminded that my faith, my hope, is very often found in what I cannot see – that is what makes it faith.

I could not see how this was good or how God would provide, or even how my future would be bright. At that moment, all I could see was the diagnosis, and it was not good. If that was where it stopped, then there was no hope. Thankfully, there were things I could not see – my future, the progress of this disease, the struggles I would have, but I also could not see His provision, His plan, His purpose, and in that I could have hope.

Even as dark as these life events had been, there was hope, and there was light in Him. "I will lift up mine eyes unto the hills – from where does my help come? My help comes from the LORD...". (Psalm 121:1-2) In spite of the darkness, in Him, I had hope. I could not see what the future would hold, but I knew He held my future, therefore, I could have hope.

Hope, in the face of darkness, is tough to find. Sometimes that darkness is so dark, it engulfs the light, and we lose sight of it. Hope becomes something we cannot see, but just because we cannot see it, does not mean it is gone or does not exist. In Him, there is always hope. It does not mean it will always be easy or free of pain, but it does mean that we can have the strength to face it and get through it because our hope and faith is in Him.

If we are honest, we all have faced hopelessness at some point in our lives. Times when we could not see the light of hope, but that is when faith is most essential. Hope is always there, even when we cannot see or feel it because our hope does not come from our circumstances – it comes from Him.

In what circumstance are you struggling to find hope? Has the darkness choked out every speck of light? Are you to the point of giving up? Remember, there is always hope, even when you cannot see it. Keep walking forward and trusting that He is there. He will never leave you or forsake you. Your hope is in the Lord, from Him will come your help. Trust Him, even when you cannot see Him. Even when darkness clouds your vision, He is there, and that is why we can still have hope.

CHAPTER 10
IT IS NOT WELL WITH MY SOUL

When peace like a river, attendeth my way,
    When sorrows like sea billows roll
Whatever my lot, thou hast taught me to say
    It is well, it is well, with my soul

It was a dark morning. Honestly, it had been a dark few months, but today was darker than most. Arriving at school, I had checked my email. I was expecting news from the doctor on another round of tests, and an email that I sent him because the current medication was not working.

For months I had watched myself decline, and I watched myself lose the ability to do one thing after another. Every night after pushing myself through work, I would collapse. Most weekends were spent in bed, trying to recoup from the week and prepare for the next one. We had been to doctor after doctor, and run test after test, and we were no closer to an answer than when we had started.

But I was hopeful. Maybe this round of tests would show something. Perhaps the doctor would finally have some answers. Maybe there was a new medication I could try. As I opened that email and began to read, I could not hold back tears. The doctor was telling me again that they had found nothing and that everything was normal. He was sorry that my current medication was not working, but he wanted me to keep trying it.

I sat there staring at the email, hoping I had read something wrong, but I had not. There was no light at the end of the tunnel, there were no answers to be found. I was sick, and getting sicker – everyone could see it – and there was nothing that we could do.

That morning we were scheduled to have devotions as a staff, but honestly, I did not want to be there. I went that morning out of simple duty, and I sat there, head down, in silence. I was fighting so hard to keep it together, and I'm sure many noticed my struggle. As the devotion time came to a close, our campus pastor began to lead us in a song, and not just any song, but a song that had been part of churches for decades, *It Is Well With My Soul*. Of all songs, did it have to be this one.

The singing began, but I could not just sit there in silence. I was the principal, and I needed to set an example. At least that is what I told myself. I started singing the first line, "When peace like a river attendeth my way, when sorrows like sea billows roll, whatever my lot...". It was right here, at this line. For the first time in my life, I could not sing this, for it was not well with my soul.

I kept trying to choke out the words as tears streamed out of my eyes, but no matter how hard I tried, I could not sing it. At that moment, everything in me was screaming at God. I was in pain, my body was failing, I was discouraged, and there seemed to be no answers coming – how could it possibly be well with my soul?
It was probably the first time that I was frank with God, and with myself, at how deeply my faith was being shaken. It was the first time in my life that no matter how hard I tried, I could not push through. Don't get me wrong, I had had many struggles before this, but none that had sidelined me this way. After almost three years of constant sickness and health issues, I could not go on any further.

And it was here that God met me. In my lowest point, He was there. I wish I could say that he waved the magic wand, and all my sickness evaporated, or that He gave me all the answers I was seeking, but He did not. In fact, I was still months away from finding a treatment that would work or having the answers I was looking for.

At this moment, though, for the first time, I finally let God know where I really was (even though He knew), and I finally admitted it to myself. Through those tears, I let God know, it was not well with my soul. I was broken, exhausted, and discouraged, but His grace was bigger. God did not condemn me for where I was, but was there to meet me at that place, and hold me when I could no longer stand.

Through that grace, I had the strength to continue. It did not mean that all of a sudden, I felt great, or that all my sorrow was gone, it merely meant that I had someone holding me, and carrying me when I could no longer walk. He loved me, and strengthened me, and gave me peace so that on the day I was given my diagnosis, as discouraging as it was, I could keep moving forward with Him in faith.

Each of us have hard days. Each of us reach a point when we want to give up, or think, "How can I keep going?" – days when it is not well with our soul. During those honest moments, God will meet us, and strengthen us and give us peace so that we can take that next step; we must simply just turn to Him. Even though every day is hard and new challenges continued to present themselves, most days, I can now honestly say it is well with my soul.

My Focus

"While we look not at the things which are seen, but at the things which are not seen; for the things which are seen are temporal, but the things which are not seen are eternal."

– II Corinthians 4:18

CHAPTER 11
MY FOCUS DETERMINES
MY REALITY

As Anakin Skywalker began his journey to become a Jedi, Qui-gon Jinn, Jedi Knight, shared one of the most profound statements I've ever heard. He very quietly reminded Anakin that his reality would be affected by what he chose to focus on. Anyone who knows me is not surprised that I would write a chapter that would include a Star Wars reference. Still, in the days after my diagnosis, this line came into my mind over and over again.

In those first few days, and honestly, weeks and months after, so many things fought for my focus. Many days I was focused on my current state of health. How was I feeling today? Were the symptoms better or worse? Was there something new that I could no longer do? How much pain was I in today? Questions, questions, and more questions were seeking my attention, with many staying in the forefront of my thoughts.

If it wasn't the current state of my health, it was my family. What is my wife thinking, and how is she coping? How are my kids holding up? Do we need to talk about this more as a family, or is silence the best thing right now? Should I ask them for help, or should I pretend that everything is okay? I can't do this _____ for my family like I use to, what should I do?

If it wasn't dwelling on family, it was the future. How are we going to pay for this latest medical bill? What are we going to do as my health deteriorates further? How will we pay for all the bills, and for the future care that is needed? Who will take care of me, and who will take care of my family in the coming days?

If it was not these things, it was work, ministry, daily chores, and hundreds of other little things. Many days it was easy for some or all of these things to consume my focus. Honestly, though, it was often as simple as how I was feeling. Was I in pain? Was I discouraged? Was I having trouble moving? Were my tremors controlled? Was I tired? All of these things were always at the forefront of my mind, and many times, these things crowded out what I really needed to be focused on.

Years ago, a pastor friend shared with me, "Pain is the great confuser." He could not have been more right. Pain and struggle can warp our perspective. They can consume our thoughts and take our energy. They can wear us down and cause us to be very hopeless. Because they are so deeply felt, they can become central to our vision, and cause us to lose perspective on what is really important.

When I am in pain, or I am discouraged, sometimes it is all I can focus on. In some ways, it becomes my whole world, and all I can see is the struggling and the pain. It consumes my focus, and when this happens, it becomes my entire reality. Everything I see, at that point, is filtered through this new reality. It colors everything I see and dictates my actions and reactions. It colors what I think and what I feel.

When this skewed perspective occurs, it causes me to lose focus of what is truly important. Instead of seeing the blessings surrounding me, I focus on the negative and the things that I do not have. Instead of an optimistic outlook, discouragement plagues me. Instead of motivation, apathy takes over.

Most importantly, though, when pain and struggle consume my focus, He is no longer in view. Instead of seeing Him, I see pain. Instead of focusing on Him, all I can see is my problems and struggles. Instead of looking to Him, I look to myself and my own strength, which I understand is failing. Instead of faith, there is only fear and doubt. When I cease to focus on Him, my hope is gone.

When this happens, my reality is most definitely changed. Instead of reacting out of faith and hope, I respond out of doubt, fear, and pain. What is the difference? My circumstances have not changed, only my perspective and focus.

It is so easy for us to lose focus on what is truly important when faced with trials and struggles, but these are the times that keeping our focus is most essential. It is during these times that He is most needed. If we lose sight of Him, we lose sight of hope. Hope will keep us going in the face of tragedy. Hope will give us strength, even when pain and fatigue are overwhelming. When He is our source, and He is our focus, our reality will change, and it will change for the better.

What are you focused on? What today is determining your reality? Is it Him? Is it your circumstances? We decide what we will focus on – no one else can determined that for us? So today, where will you choose to place your focus? Always remember, your focus really does determine your reality.

CHAPTER 12
A HEAVEN OF HELL OR
A HELL OF HEAVEN

Am I still a good father? How do I still function as a husband? How can I still be a good dad and husband? Am I putting too much on them and others? Am I still being a good friend? How can I keep up at work? Question after question after question pours through my mind, and doubts swirl. Once again, I am left wondering these and so many other questions, trapped in the "hell" of my mind.

Chronic disease affects so many physical aspects of a person's life. It limits what a person can do. It fills your body with pain and discomfort. It brings exhaustion from the simplest tasks, and it drains so much physically from you. If it stopped there, that would be enough, but it does not.

John Milton once wrote, "The mind is its own place and in itself, can make a heaven of hell, a hell of heaven." Aside from the physical pain, and the physical toll it takes on your body, the mental anguish is sometimes worse. The mind, I have found, is a constant battle. Fear, doubt, uncertainty, sadness, and so many other thoughts and emotions regularly parade through your mind, and you are left battling thoughts that will not end.

Mine's Parkinson's, What's Yours?

Some of these thoughts are real and legitimate; others are pure manifestations of fears, doubt, and pain. It is so easy to, in a sense, take a trip "Down the Rabbit Hole" and end up in places you never intended or wanted. Regardless of whether or not your life is pleasant or a struggle, the mental anguish that disease brings along with it, truly changes so many things in a person's life from a "Heaven to Hell."

It causes one to imagine the worst-case scenario, and doubt every aspect of your life. How can my spouse love me with this? Can I be the father my children need? Am I able to provide and keep working? It messes with your self-image, body image, and any "image" of yourself that you can think of. Even things that are not affected by this disease, are in some ways changed due to the battle raging in your mind.

So many times I have battled the new place I have in my family. I have the most wonderful, supportive, and loving wife, but I see the things I cannot do, and I struggle and doubt. I love her, and she loves me, but the doubts and pain I face cause me to withdraw and imagine the worst. Even though our relationship is so much more than the things missing, too often, it becomes my singular focus – my battleground in my mind. In this, I do not give her the credit she has shown over and over again, and I short-change the love that not only brought us together but keeps us as one.

I look at my children and the love we have for each other. I see the compassion they show me and all the ways they help me. Yet once again, I know the burden they face, and all their father cannot do, and once again, doubts creep in. Even though they never focus on the things they miss, it often fills my mind.

I see friends around me, and I see people who care for me and I for them. I see bonds that go back for years, and I see all the things we once were able to do together. I now see the things I cannot do, and how things have changed because of this illness, and it hurts, and many times consumes my vision.

These same things could be said for work, family, ministry – on and on the list goes, and all I can see is the "hell" that is my life. This perspective can be all-consuming. It can cause you to withdraw even further, and it colors everything you see. It discourages and becomes a self-fulfilling prophecy.

This week was especially discouraging for me because this became my focus. All I could see was the "hell" of my circumstances. I saw things I could not do, things that were now missing in my life, decisions I was now having to make, and struggles I was having in so many areas. It caused me to doubt and wonder about the future, about relationships, and about myself and others around me. In these thoughts, the hurt and pain consumed me, and it was all I could see. I was in tears most days, I hurt those closest to me, and I was so discouraged.

In conversations with others, but especially my wife, she continued to love me (in spite of the hurt I was spewing at her and others). She showed me that so much of my struggle was simply "me being stuck in my head." Were these things I was feeling real – yes, but really not the all-consuming, all-encompassing things I thought they were. She reminded me that our relationship and my life were and are so much more than these difficulties.

When you are stuck in this mindset, it is hard to will yourself out of it. During this week, my bride showed me that these doubts, fears, discouragement, and pain only defined me if I allowed them to. These things were only all-encompassing if I allowed them to be. Through her love, care, and patience, she showed me what I really needed to see. She helped me realize that I decide if the "hell" of all my physical struggles will really be a "heaven or hell" here on Earth.

Without her love and the love of others, I am not sure in what place I would be. When we are in the "hell" of our thinking, we need others around us that can help us really see not only reality but hope. It may be overwhelming, it may be difficult, it may affect so many things, but it only affects your mind and spirit if you allow it. Don't get me wrong, we all have bad days and weeks, and I know I will have many more in the future, but I also have people around me who will fight to keep me out of that place.

Have you ever been in a position like this? Have you ever been consumed by the pain you are feeling? What did you do to "right the ship" of your thinking? Whether you are fighting chronic illness in your life or not, we all have struggles and pain that threaten to overwhelm us, as they did for me this week. When this happens, we need to see it for what is it. We need to remember that our pain and struggle is only half of the battle. What we think and dwell on concerning that pain and suffering is often more critical, and will have more effect on our fight than even the pain we are suffering.

What is threatening to consume your thinking right now? What thinking is making a "hell" of your situation? Whatever it is, remember, you may not be able to control the circumstance, you may not be able to ease the pain. Still, you can decide what you will think about it and how you will face it. Regardless of whether or not you are walking through heaven or hell here on Earth, you and your thinking will decide if it is really heaven or if it is hell.

CHAPTER 13
SLEEPLESS NIGHTS

It's 4 a.m. Once again, I lie here, staring into the dark. It has only been 3 ½ hours since I drifted off to sleep. By yesterday, the end of the week, I was so exhausted I couldn't keep my eyes open, yet here I am, after barely 3 hours of sleep, lying wide awake.

Unfortunately, this is almost a nightly description of what happens. No matter when I go to sleep, no matter how exhausted I am, I can look forward to 4, maybe 5 hours of sleep if I am lucky. As I lay there wide awake at 4 o'clock, I know that by about 2 or 3 in the afternoon, I will once again be exhausted, deciding if I need to nap or to just push through. No matter what I choose, or how tired I am, I have a glorious 4 hours of sleep awaiting me.

To say it is frustrating, might be the understatement of the year. As I have begun this journey, I have learned that this is one of the joyous symptoms of Parkinson's disease that most patients battle with. It is a cruel twist of irony that when rest is so essential, it alludes the individuals who need it most. No matter how long I lie there, the result is going to be the same – I will be wide awake.

Mine's Parkinson's, What's Yours?

So many mornings, I would lie there and be frustrated and aggravated that sleep would not come, which would do nothing for me, except put me in an excellent mood for the day.

One morning as I was lying there, aggravated once again that I could not sleep, I started thinking of the people around me. The Lord simply impressed on my heart to take a few moments and pray for them. Many mornings it would surprise me the people that I thought of. People were brought to mind that I had not thought of in years. Sometimes it was people who were going through difficulties, or I knew only through my online support groups that I prayed for.

As I lay there in the dark, I would quietly pray – sometimes it was a general prayer (especially if I did not know a specific need). Sometimes it was a particular prayer for strength or for a need that someone had. After I would do this for a while, I would walk downstairs, and just begin to write (which is how this blog got started).

Was my lack of sleep frustrating – absolutely, in some ways, it still is, but I had a choice. I could be frustrated and aggravated all day and accomplished nothing, or I could take this frustration and turn it into something useful and good.

You see, we all have frustrations. We all have things that we wish we could change, big and small. Do I wish I could get more sleep – most definitely! Do I try things to help me get more sleep – many times. Yet even as I work to change this, I still have this daily choice. I can let my frustrations and challenges rule me, or I can, in a sense, take control of these circumstances, and find something good and useful in them.

Do I always have the right attitude – no. Do I sometimes get aggravated still – sure I do, I am human. But the longer I walk this journey, the more I realize this is a daily choice. Every day I will be presented with this choice, and it is my choice alone what I do with it. All I can do is take this one day at a time, and today I choose not

Charles E. Mickles Jr.

to be aggravated, but look for a way to turn this frustration into something useful.

CHAPTER 14
SOME DAYS I FEEL LIKE FRODO BAGGINS

I wish this had never happened to me. How many times have I thought that in my life, and especially during this last month? I wish this had never come to me. I'm sure I am not the only one who has felt this way. Whether it's a chronic illness, a significant loss, or other life events, at one time or another, we all think this.

The other day, I was watching one of my favorite movies, *The Lord of the Rings: The Fellowship of the Ring*. If you have never watched these movies or read the books, you don't know what you are missing. They are long movies, but worth the time to watch them. There are so many beautiful moments and narratives. Frodo Baggins, the main character, is set upon a path that he never wanted to travel (sound familiar?).

Feeling discouraged and overwhelmed with the weight of this journey, he has a conversation with his mentor, Gandolf. In exhaustion, and even some fear, Frodo simply tells Gandolf that he wished none of this had ever happened. He did not want the ring and the burden that came with it. Have you ever been in a place like this? I certainly have; in fact, it often felt like I lived there.

Frodo never asked for this path. He never wanted to bear this burden. This challenging and difficult journey was thrust upon him. As I have dealt with problem after problem (arthritis, emergency surgery, the loss of my sister, cancer battles/health issues in the family, and now Parkinson's), many days, I have felt like Frodo. I have wished that none of this ever happened.

That's how Frodo put it, and that's how I felt. God, why me? Why now; I'm only 44? I wish this had never happened. These are some of the conversations I had with God and others. Unfortunately, very few answers and reasons were given. But if you keep watching the movie, the discussion does not stop there.

Gandolf simply reminds him that there is a plan and purpose to our lives, that there is someone there for us, watching us, helping us, and that, more than anything, is an encouraging thought. Psalm 23 reminds us, "Even though I walk through the valley of the shadow of death, I will fear no evil, for you are with me." I find myself very literally walking this path, but I need not fear, for He is with me.

He also gives one simple reminder, a small piece of advice. He reminds Frodo that the only thing we have to decide is what we will ultimately do with the time we are given. What will we use it for? We do not know how many days we have before us, or what they will be like, but we can decide how we will walk through them, and how we will face this new and challenging journey.

Parkinson's is the "ring" I have been given to bear. All of us have a ring – what is yours? While we do not often choose the ring we will carry, we can choose how we will bear it. We decide, day by day, what to do with the time we are given. What will you do with this journey and the time you have been given? He is with us, He knows the path and its end, and if we let Him, He will guide and comfort us, and that is an encouraging thought.

CHAPTER 15
WHAT'S REALLY IMPORTANT

So many things jockey for our attention every day, often every moment. So many things that seem necessary. So many things we feel we cannot live without. So many things that, at the time, seem so important, but are they really?

Tragedy, pain, and challenges all have a way of making things in life crystal clear. These difficulties strip away the unimportant and help us see what truly matters. The first time this happened to me was after my sister, at the age of 25, passed away very suddenly from brain cancer. It is something I would never wish on anyone, and it was one of the most painful experiences I have ever walked through.

The loss and the void that this event left behind is something that, to this day, I still feel. In the days and months after her passing, it surprised me how so many things that I thought were so important, really did not seem that important anymore. Something that just days, weeks, and months before had seemed so vital, just did not rank where it had.

It was as if something, even more critical overshadowed them. As time moved on, this feeling and experience seemed to grow smaller.

Once again, things, that in reality, were far less critical, began to crowd out what was truly special and consequential in my life. I allowed less essential items to take the place of what really should have priority.

After learning of this new challenge of Parkinson's, I spent a lot of time in silence, processing, talking to God, and considering what my future held. As I looked at my life, I realized that most likely, I had fewer days ahead, fewer days that I would be functional before me. I began to ask and consider, "What is really important? What is worth my time and energy? What should my focus be? What things have I let slip that I should not have?"

As I considered these things, I began to see relationships that I had neglected. I saw times I was not intentional. I recognized issues that I got worked up and frustrated over really were not that important. I began to see so many wasted opportunities. I saw things that were much more important in my life than they should have been. I realized that important things – family, friends, relationships, helping others – were taking a backseat. I saw myself having a casual attitude towards these things and not being intentional.

What was really important? Where should my focus be in the latter half of my life? What would I choose to emphasize? What would I focus my time and energy upon, and once again make a priority in my life? With this disease, what would be most important? What opportunities were missed or wasted simply because I was too busy or too tired (because I was spending my time and energy on less important things)?

We have such a finite time to live and make a difference, which is something this disease has reminded me of. Over the last month, I have spent a lot of time simply asking, what am I doing with the time I have been given? We have so many opportunities, so much that we miss that is truly important. Why is that? Why do we major on the minor things of life?

Mine's Parkinson's, What's Yours?

Many times it is because our perspective becomes skewed, and we think that the wrong things are really the most important. We fail to take a step back and really ask ourselves, "Is this really that important, is this really where my focus and time should be placed?" If we were honest, most of the time, we would have to answer "no."

We have such a limited amount of time before us. What do you consider most important – is that really most important in your life? What gets your time, energy, and emotions? It is easy to lose focus, get off track, and let other things crowd out what is essential. As I spent time quietly considering these things, I realized how off I had become, and the need I had to discover once again what was truly important. What I found was how many things, in light of this new life circumstance, were not as important as I thought they were just a few months before.

I wish I could say that I lived this perfectly, but I am still learning, as are we all. What is your focus in life? Are you spending time on the things that are truly most important? This is something I am learning to consider day by day with the time I have left. What will you focus on? Take time to consider this, and then go after it with all you have.

CHAPTER 16
IT REALLY IS A
WONDERFUL LIFE

"No man is a failure who has friends."

This year has felt different. I don't know if it is my diagnosis, or simply how my body feels, but this Christmas has a different meaning for me. Maybe it is just my changed perspective, but like George Bailey, I am seeing things differently than I have before.

Nothing says Christmas quite like the movie. *It's A Wonderful Life*. As a child, I probably watched this movie 100 times every year. It seemed to play on a continuous loop during December. If you have never seen it (although I do not know how that is possible), it is a touching tale of a man who is discouraged. Yet, with the help of his guardian angel, he sees how his life has impacted others. As the movie ends, he sees that impact as hundreds of people rush to help him in his time of need.

This year marks the first time in 5 years that I have written anything. I am not sure why I stopped, but I know why I started again. I was challenged this year with the question, "How will your suffering be used?" For me, I have begun writing with the hope of helping others through their struggles. To comfort others out of my pain and struggle and encourage them not to give up.

This year, I began looking through things I had written previously and came across a post about this movie that I had written back in 2014. It amazed me how much this year mirrored that year and the experiences I walked through. Below is an excerpt:

As many of you know, this year was a difficult one for my health – in April, at 39 years of age, I was told I would have my 3rd hip replacement. I later also found out I had an infection. In addition to the health problems, finances were tight, stress was placed on my family, I was out of work, and in general, it all was overwhelming. Many times, I felt like I was at the end of my rope.

As I watch It's A Wonderful Life, it was like I was watching the movie for the first time. I saw and understood George Bailey in a way I never had before. I saw myself in that man – a man so overwhelmed that he almost gave up, and then Clarence showed up, and his perspective changed. When he returned home, with a different outlook, the second miracle occurred – George saw an outpouring of love and care he had never witnessed. Friends, family, and ordinary people gave and cared for him in an amazing way.

While that closing scene played, tears began streaming down my face as memory after memory flooded back to me from this past year. Memories of people bringing us meals. Memories of gifts that covered every medical bill and then some. Memories of people taking care of housework – cleaning, cutting grass, home repairs. Memories of people praying over me and lifting my family up before him. From cards, visits, gifts, and just caring in every way imaginable, I watched as people surrounded us. They cared for us in one of our darkest hours and most significant times of need.

The tears I shed 2 days ago watching that priceless movie were not tears of sorrow, but of overwhelming joy and thankfulness. Thankfulness for so many that surrounded my family and me and cared for us in so many ways. Gratitude for seeing God use so many to provide for us in an amazing way. Thankfulness for showing true His promise that He would never leave or forsake us.

Charles E. Mickles Jr.

As I sat, wiping away the tears, so many names came to mind, so many instances that showed His love through the people around me. Was it hard? Yes. Do I want to go through it again? Not particularly. Were there very discouraging and dark days? Absolutely. Is it sometimes still hard? Yes. Am I thankful? Beyond expression. I saw very clearly — more clearly than I ever have — what George Bailey learned in that beautiful movie. I was humbled and blessed by so many of you during our need.

As I read over these words from 5 years ago, I realized that once again, I found myself in this same dark place. A place of very little hope, facing a battle I most likely would eventually lose. Many days were a struggle, and there were many times I was weary of the fight. But just like George, I had something extraordinary, something that would give strength as I walked this path. I had friends, family really, who were with me. I had a physical and online community surrounding my family and me and holding us up.

Once again this year, I have seen so many come alongside my family to hold us up, strengthen us, and bless us. These people have provided rays of hope in very dark times, and have given us the strength to keep going just a little while longer. Like George Bailey, I have been reminded that no matter the struggle, there is hope, and there are ones who will always be there to walk with us. We have been reminded of God's love through the community surrounding us.

No matter how dark the days become, or how hard the road is to walk, I have hope. I have been reminded that even with this terrible disease and the struggles that come with it, it really is a "Wonderful Life." My prayer for us all this season, "The Lord bless you and keep you; and make His face shine upon you and be gracious to you...and give you peace." (Numbers 6:24-26). May you and your family truly be blessed, even as you walk through the struggles of this life.

CHAPTER 17
PAIN IS THE GREAT CONFUSER

Pain, the first thing I am greeted with every morning (if I have actually slept). Pain, the last thing I feel when and if I drift off to sleep. My constant companion each and every day. It is the "white noise" that fills every moment, and it is something I can never separate myself from.

Chronic illness, in most cases, equals some form of chronic pain. Having battled Arthritis since the age of 15, and now Parkinson's Disease, constant pain has been part of my life for over 30 years. So long have I experienced this that I honestly do not remember what it feels like not to have pain. If you had something, good or bad, that you experienced for as long as you could remember, you would probably feel the same way.

Even on good days, days when I am feeling pretty good, pain is still a constant. This pain causes fatigue and requires much more time and effort to accomplish the most basic tasks. Dealing with this day in and day out is exhausting, and can wear on a person not just physically, but mentally, emotionally, and spiritually.

With a companion that is so constant, the toll that this can take on a person can be huge. Because it is always there, it can consume your thoughts, and the exhaustion from dealing with it can fray your emotions. As you deal with it more and more, it can cause you to question your faith. All of this adds up to, at times, a rather drastic change in perspective.

Things that seemed logical and straightforward before, now are overshadowed and confused by what you are feeling each day. It changes your perception of things and can cause you to see things much differently. This can be good. It can strengthen your determination, drive, and help you be more compassionate and caring.

The flip side to this, though, is that it can also cause depression, loneliness, sadness, and a feeling of being overwhelmed. When this happens, it can cause an individual to give up and stop trying. It can cause anger, discouragement, and confusion.

When this has happened in my life, I have found myself solely focused on this — to the point where it overshadowed everything else. It made the most basic decisions, ones I questioned, and it caused me to view things in a way that was not correct because all I could feel and see was the pain.

As this consumed my thoughts to the exclusion of everything else, my focus stopped being the Lord, or the good around me. Instead, I saw pain and discouragement, and began to view life through this prism. In turn, this affected how I felt, how I saw things in general, and how I made decisions.

The confusion it brings is not always easy to deal with, and the viewpoint it gives you, while sometimes helpful and useful, is most times, not so much so. When you couple that with stress, fatigue, and the hopelessness of it never stopping, sometimes seeing things as they really are is challenging. It is no wonder people fighting this sometimes just give up. This is something I never understood until

Mine's Parkinson's, What's Yours?

I personally battled it for so long. As you battle this pain, getting out of your own head is probably the hardest part.

That, more than ever, is when faith, family, and friends (the 3 f's) are so critical. If I do not have that outside perspective, I get trapped in my mind and thinking, and my viewpoint is totally skewed. These outside voices help keep me grounded and see reality for what it is.

Instead of my whole world being overshadowed and consumed by pain, it is relegated to a manageable part of me, and not something that destroys me. Pain does not have to be physical to have this effect. Emotional and mental pain often operate the same way.

No matter the type of pain, we need people around us that will help us keep things in perspective and encourage us in the fight. As I have battled this for 30 years, I have had to decide if I would control or define my pain, or if my pain would control and define me. Honestly, I have been in both places.

Each day I decide which it will be. Each day, the people around me with love and encouragement help me keep this in perspective. No one is immune from pain. The questions is, will you control it, or will it control you? Instead of letting it confuse you and become your sole focus, allow this pain to strengthen you to keep fighting. Let it soften you to care more for others. Allow it to deepen your faith in the One that will sustain you and walk with you through the pain.

When this happens, your pain changes your perspective and helps you as you take this journey. Instead of pain becoming the great confuser, it becomes a great helper to you as you walk the path before you.

Well, This Stinks

"I have told you these things, so that in me you may have peace. In this world you will have trouble. But take heart! I have overcome the world." – John 16:33

CHAPTER 18
THAT LIFE STINKS BUCKET IS GETTING PRETTY FULL

As a young man, I thought the bucket was full after my arthritis diagnosis (silly boy). Surely it was full after emergency stomach surgery and a hip replacement by 19. No, well definitely after my sister passed from cancer, and my dad had cancer (not to mention my wife's complicated pregnancies). Still not full, even after 2 more hip replacements – how big was this bucket?

This is how I felt. Time after time, more and more got poured into the "Life Stinks Bucket." I really was beginning to wonder if it was more like a swimming pool than a bucket, because there was no way a bucket could hold this much.

In spite of all of this, I was still upbeat and generally saw the good in life. Surely by now, I had weathered most of the challenges life could throw at me, and maybe things would settle down. Apparently, that was not the plan, and that "Life Stinks Bucket" was about to get a little more full.

When the doctor told me I had Parkinson's, I sat there in some disbelief, thinking, "This totally stinks." How could this be? I had already had enough to fill 4 or 5 "Life Stinks Buckets". How could I fit any more in this bucket? As we walked out, teary-eyed, I remember saying to my wife, "That life stinks bucket is getting pretty full." This is how I really felt and was probably one of the most truthful statements that I had ever uttered.

It was easy at that moment to focus on all the bad, all that was wrong, and see a bleak future with little hope. I could picture all the ways my body would fail me, and the struggles that I not only had, but would have, and the pain it would cause those I loved. It was easy to look at this mountain of sorrow and simply exclaim, "This stinks."

You see, at that moment, all I could focus on, all that I could see, was the sorrow and pain. From that vantage point, life really did stink. But you know, I was missing something important. I had another bucket. I was missing all the good – all the blessings surrounding me. There were so many things to be thankful for, so much good and so many blessings.

The bad things, this new challenge, did not negate all the good, but at that moment, it skewed my perspective and clouded my vision. It overshadowed all that was still good and made me forget how truly blessed I was. As I thought and prayed about this, the Lord began to remind me of these things, and that "Life Stink Bucket", didn't seem quite so full after all.

This revelation did not mean the pain and sorrow were gone. It did not say there was no fear for the future or that my body was magically healed. It merely meant that the bad, the sorrow, was not my sole focus. There were many good things – things to be thankful for – and this was just one more challenge to make life a little more interesting.

We all have a "Life Stinks Bucket", but we also have a bucket full of blessings. We can choose which bucket to carry with us daily. It does not mean we do not acknowledge the pain and struggle. It just simply means we choose not to be consumed by it. Jeremiah 17:7 reminds us, "...blessed is the one who trusts in the Lord, whose confidence is in Him." No matter how full that life stinks bucket gets, if I am trusting in Him, I will be blessed, and that bucket will always outweigh the sorrows of life.

CHAPTER 19
GOD, THIS PLAN REALLY STINKS

So, let me see if I have this right Lord: I need to have yet another struggle? Is my arthritis not enough? The pain and death of my sister to cancer is not enough? My continuing health struggles and the burden it places on my family in every possible way is not sufficient? So "the plan" is to give me an even more significant, life-altering disease – one with no cure, that will just get worse over time and make life even more difficult? This is the plan? Well, as far as I can see, this plan stinks!

I do not know how many of you have ever had a conversation like this with God, but I have a few times in my life, and this summer was one of those times. It was quite possibly one of the most honest conversations I ever had with God. It was not a conversation had disrespectfully, but a conversation borne out of utter bewilderment. This plan seemed utterly insane. As I said in the previous chapter, that "Life Stinks Bucket" was already overflowing. How could it be a good plan to lay one more struggle on my family and me?

I was really starting to believe that Murphy's Law (Anything that can go wrong will go wrong.) must be real and that my last name must actually have been Murphy. "How in the world, God, is giving me one more challenge, one more difficulty, a good plan?" I looked around at things as I was processing this new news, and I thought, "This really stinks. God, your plan stinks."

I know that this is not the most Christian viewpoint, but in my heart, at that moment, that is what I was thinking – God, your plan stinks. This new health issue was causing more struggle and burden in EVERY area of life, and it made me weary. "There must be a mistake, God. This can't be right." It all seemed so wrong.

If many of us were honest, at some point, we have had some version of this conversation with God. In life, we want things to make sense. We want to know and understand the reasons things happen. We want to see the little pieces fit together perfectly to show the beautiful picture of our life. Often, that is not the case. We have been given all the pieces of our life and are trying to put this puzzle together. Unfortunately, we are unable to see the picture on the box.

We cannot see how these pieces fit together. No matter how hard we try to fit them together, they won't fit, it does not make sense, and it is frustrating. We try to pound and push them into place, but no matter how hard we try, we still can't understand why this piece is part of our life, because it does not seem to make sense with everything else.

As I sat and had this conversation over and over with God (and some days I still do), I realized that I may never understand why I now have Parkinson's. Just like I still did not know why I had arthritis, or my sister passed away, or my dad had cancer, or why over and over again, more challenges were added.

Sometimes, I might catch a glimpse and see some good that came from these and other events, but I would still be left thinking, "God, couldn't you do this another way?" While this new challenge

Charles E. Mickles Jr.

definitely stunk, not knowing and understanding stunk even more. Most likely, I will never know (this side of heaven) why this was God's plan, and from my human perspective, it stinks. But in this, I must remember, there is a different, eternal perspective, and He is in control.

So basically, I am once again left with the question, "Can I trust Him?" When His plan, in my eyes, stinks and makes ZERO sense, will I trust Him? The reality of life is that some things stink, and in those moments that do not make sense, will I have the faith to say, "God, this stinks. I don't understand, but I will keep walking forward and trusting you."

What things in your life "stink" right now? In spite of it, can you trust Him as you walk through it? When, in our eyes, God's plan seems crazy, we must seek Him all the more and believe that no matter how insane the plan looks or feels, He is in control, and He is with us through every step. We may not "know" understanding, but we can "know" Him, and if we know Him, we can trust that He understands and will help us take each step, one day at a time.

CHAPTER 20
PLANNING FOR THE UNTHINKABLE

"This disease could progress slowly or quickly. You could be able to work for 5 more years or 20. Everyone that has Parkinson's progresses differently." This is what our doctor told us the day I was diagnosed. How in the world do we plan for something so unpredictable?

In reality, my life was now no more unpredictable than it was a few moments before, but it sure felt that way. So many questions raced through my mind, but the main problem I had was, how will I provide for my family? What happens if I can only work for a few more years? How will we survive?

As we started looking for resources, we came upon one thing after another that we needed to do or decide, and none of them were enjoyable. I was only 44 for crying out loud; this is the last thing I should be thinking about at this age – or at least that is what I thought.

Our first stop was a visit with an Elder Care Lawyer (yes, that is as fun as it sounds). As we sat in his office, we talked about our future and how to plan. What if I stop working in 5 years? What if I need to go onto disability? What about Medicaid? What if I become bedridden and need round the clock care? (I know – what exciting discussions for a young man and his wife to be having – not)

But it did not stop there. Next, we had to begin to consider, beyond power of attorney, what things needed now to be in my wife's name, and how soon did she need to take these things over. As a man, it was emasculating. Slowly, piece by piece, I was having to give up everything I had worked so hard for. I even had to give her my Star Wars and record collections! If you know me – you know how hard that was! Don't get me wrong; I knew these steps needed to be taken and that these things needed to be done, but it was no fun. I was so glad I could do this to provide for my family, but it was still hard.

I realized when talking with my counselor that it felt like I was giving up. It was like I was throwing in the towel and admitting defeat. I was grieving the loss of, really everything, and while it was hard, it also felt good.

As I sat by my wife and began to sign things over to her control, while challenging, it was good. This is the rollercoaster that chronic disease often puts you on. I love my family, and as hard as this was, there was nothing more loving that I could do for them. And because of that love, I was glad to do it. It still hurt, but it also gave a feeling of joy that I could give these gifts to those I loved.

In spite of this turmoil of emotions, I stood back and realized that regardless of our plans, our trust still must be focused squarely on Him. My life was just as uncertain today as it was yesterday, and these plans, while wise, could not protect us from everything that was coming. Alongside this planning, our focus and trust needed to be Him. As uncertain as this disease is, and as hard as these decisions are, He is constant, He has a plan, and He will care for us in every way, and that is an encouraging thought.

CHAPTER 21
SAD, DISCOURAGED, AND DEPRESSED, BUT STILL TRUSTING GOD

This year, more than many others, has been discouraging. Being hit by one trial after another was, in many ways, depressing. The mourning and grief that came with this was sometimes more than one could bear. If I am trusting you, God, how can I be depressed or discouraged – does that mean I am not trusting or that my faith is not strong?

This last question has rattled around my mind and heart so many times as we walked through this year. I remember hearing from different religious people the idea that being depressed or discouraged meant your faith and trust were not in God. Sure, you could be sad, because that is a natural emotion, but if you were truly trusting God, depression and discouragement were not part of your life.

Last year started with my doctor looking at me, and simply saying, "Maybe you are just depressed, and that is what is causing your symptoms." Inside, I rolled my eyes and thought, "Yeah, right," but

I went along with it. I humored him and thought, "I'm trusting God, I'm not depressed."

When I went to the psychiatrist, and we started talking, boy was I surprised. She looked at me and said, "You can actually get out of bed each day and go to work?" She then shared that most people, battling what I battle, can't do that. Based on what she was seeing and hearing, I was battling depression (which we later discovered was a natural part of Parkinson's and the loss of dopamine producers in the brain).

We began to treat this in conjunction with Parkinson's, and I realized that I had been battling this for some time. I did not see it because I did not even give it a consideration. I'm generally upbeat, and look on the bright side of things, but inside, I was really struggling – more than most people or even I knew.

So here I was, battling yet another aspect of this spectacular disease. I remember talking with God and asking him how I could be discouraged, depressed, and ready to give up some days if I was truly trusting Him. To me, it seemed a very odd combination, and in some ways seemed at odds with the other.

In answer, I was directed to a Bible story I knew very well. Yet, now, I saw it differently than I ever had before. This past fall, my Bible study leader voluntold me and some other men that we were going to take turns teaching (thank you, Jason). Without really looking at it, I volunteered for the story of Elijah. As I studied and prepared, I had the answer to my earlier question.

You see, Elijah, a great prophet of God, had just defeated the 450 prophets of Baal. Yet when he was threatened by the queen, he fled in despair. Throughout the encounter, you see the discouragement, you see the depression, and you hear a man ready to give up. Had he stopped trusting God or following him? In reading this, I don't think so.

Mine's Parkinson's, What's Yours?

Never once did he say he no longer believed in or trusted God. Never once did he refuse to obey or give God the silent treatment. As he did speak with God, one thing was evident – things were not working out like Elijah thought they should, and for him, it was discouraging. He was still following God, but he was weary and, in some ways, tired of the fight.

Did this mean he was not trusting God? I can't say for sure, but as I read this, I still see a man of faith. I see a man ready to follow God's leading, but he is tired and does not understand. In that moment, I saw myself in this prophet. This year, I have never doubted God, or that He had a plan. I trusted Him, but I was weary, and this latest health challenge just did not make sense.

I was discouraged and grieving so many things. I was depressed thinking of what my health was like and would be like in the future. I was heartbroken for my family. Did I stop following God or doubt Him? No, I fully believed that He was in control and had a plan. I just did not particularly like this plan, and I grieved the path I had to walk.

My depression, discouragement, and grief did not mean I stopped trusting God. It only meant I was tired and worn and did not want to walk this path. These are all things I shared with Him, and He met me where I was. Imagine if I had waited to "have it all together" before I approached Him?

Over this year, I have learned to trust God more deeply. While I do not like His plan right now, I wholeheartedly believe that He is with me and will direct and provide. I am still discouraged some days. I am still in the grieving process, and there are days where I am depressed about my future. Yet even with those feelings, I trust Him, and as much as I do not like where He has me, I know He is with me. He sees my sorrow and struggle, and He meets me where I am and helps me walk forward. Thankfully, He is with me, and no matter how hard or discouraging this path gets, even in discouragement, I will trust Him.

Letting Go

Do not be anxious about anything, but in every situation, by prayer and petition, with thanksgiving, present your requests to God. And the peace of God, which transcends all understanding, will guard your hearts and minds in Christ Jesus. – Philippians 4:6-7

CHAPTER 22
PLAYING "THAT" CARD

"Really, you are going to make the person with Parkinson's, the person with arthritis and 3 hip replacements do that?" My daughter just stood there staring at me, "Wow, dad, you really going to play the Parkinson's card?" I smiled, "Absolutely sweetheart, there's got to be some benefits to this."

This conversation has played out half a dozen times, with various people, not just my daughter. I love saying it to my wife, especially when there's a job around the house that I do not want to do. It is funny, when I say this, I usually get one of three reactions. First, some people just bust out laughing, because they know me and they're not really surprised I would say it. The second reaction I get is just a blank stare, because people are surprised that I would say it. For those who know me best, they just respond "whatever."

As you can guess, this is often said very tongue-in-cheek, and often said in a joking way, especially when I want to get out of doing something. Even though it's a joke, and at that moment I'm not saying it seriously, there is some truth to it.

Growing up, I had many difficulties and challenges physically. Diagnosed with arthritis at an early age, undergoing numerous surgeries as a teenager, and having my first hip replacement at 19, I was no stranger to challenges. I have always had the philosophy, though, of pushing through. I did not want anything to stop me, and I often wore as a badge of pride, the fact that I could do so many things in spite of my physical difficulties. No matter what, I was not going to let my physical struggles hold me back or keep me from doing something.

Parkinson's, though, stopped me dead in my tracks. In the years leading up to my diagnosis, I started to experience more and more difficulties. Still, the year right before my diagnosis hit me like a ton of bricks. I got to the point that no matter how hard I tried, I just could not do things like I wanted to. I was having trouble writing, typing, driving, walking, and just getting around in general. I would push and push myself, but no matter how hard I tried, I just could not do some things, and I would collapse each night utterly exhausted.

It was a very humbling experience, and at times very frustrating. There were so many things I wanted to do with my family, at work, in my ministry, but no matter how hard I tried, I just could not do it. I would spend every weekend in bed recuperating from the week, many times wondering how I would go on. For someone who took such pride in all he could do, in spite of his physical challenges, it was very humbling, frustrating, and discouraging.

In those moments, God showed me that I can't do everything. Whether because of my physical condition or just the fact of getting older, every day, my body was getting weaker. Sometimes no matter how hard I wanted to, I just could not do it. I realized it is okay to play that card. I can tell others I can't do it. It is fine to let some of these things go.

When I could let go of my pride and just admit that I couldn't do it all, a weight was lifted off my shoulders – a weight that I had put there. It was the weight of expectations, the weight of pride, the weight of what other people would think – weights that I did not need to be carrying. It is okay not to do everything. It is okay to admit that you can't do it all, and it is okay to simply say no.

Thankfully, after my diagnosis, the doctors have found treatments that have helped immensely, and given me back many of the things I've lost this last year. However, I realize there will come times when I still cannot do (or should not be doing) things. I wish I could say that I don't still struggle with this. I wish I could say that I have no problem saying no (no comments from those who know me). Each day presents new challenges, and some days I do better with this than others, but I am learning. I don't play the Parkinson's card every day. Still, I'm beginning to become more comfortable letting go and just saying I can't, and when I do, I realize that it is okay.

CHAPTER 23
THE "HANDICAP" PLACARD

Sitting in the doctor's office, having just heard the news, still stunned, I look over at my wife, and she gives me an encouraging smile. She looks at me and says to the doctor and me, "Now I know this is going to make you upset, Honey...," and right there, I knew where this was going.

In marriage, it is not unusual to have the same discussions over and over again, especially if, in these discussions, there is some disagreement. Over the years, due to my arthritis and then Parkinson's, I had struggled physically getting around. Sometimes walking was very painful and challenging, but I was not going to let it stop me. I was going to push through and show myself and everyone around me that this was not going to keep me down. I did not need help (I often very arrogantly thought).

Every time my struggles became more challenging, the subject would be brought up to my doctors and me. "Ched, maybe it is time to get a handicap placard for the times when you are struggling and need it." When this was said, my blood pressure and anger would rise. I would adamantly shut down the conversation before it began by simply declaring, "I don't need that, end of discussion."

Mine's Parkinson's, What's Yours?

In reality, I did need it, but instead of accepting help, my pride stood in the way. In many situations, I refused to ask for and accept help, at times fighting vigorously against it. I was determined to "Do it myself" (as my daughter at the age of 2 often told us). One thing this last year had begun to show me was that many times, I could not do it myself. No matter how hard I pushed or how deep my desire was, I simply physically could not do it.

Frustration and anger would soon follow, and sometimes, I would try to do it, even when I knew I should not or could not. During this year, many people have fussed at me for this (and honestly sometimes still do because I am hardheaded). God has begun to deal with this pride and helped me realize it is okay to ask for and receive help. It does not make me less of a person, it does not mean I am weak, it does not mean I'm needy or a burden. It merely means I need help, as we all sometimes do.

Why do we find it so hard to admit this and ask for help? I don't know, but many times it is pride. It is a stubborn determination to show the world no weakness or need, and simply "do it myself."

So here came the question, the question I had been so adamantly fighting against for years. My wife looked at the doctor and said, "I know this is going to make you mad Honey, but should we get him a handicap tag for his bad days?" She was braced for an argument, but none came. I simply looked at her and said, "It's okay Honey, I'm not going to fight you about this anymore. Maybe it is time, and maybe I do need this help."

Honestly, it was kind of funny to see the small look of surprise on her face. Maybe I was finally learning the lesson God had for so long been trying to teach me. You cannot always do it by yourself, and sometimes we all need help. Also, it was very freeing, because I did not have to keep bearing the burden by myself that I was never meant to carry. I cannot say that I am entirely living this out; after all, I am a stubborn man, but God is showing me this need in my life, and I am finally learning it is okay.

I need help sometimes, and I need to accept the loving, caring gestures given to me by those around me. My dad told me long ago, "Never deny someone the opportunity to serve and bless you. When you do, you rob them of the opportunity and blessing of serving God through serving you." It has taken a while, but I am finally beginning to understand this.

I've also realized, those around me are dealing with pain and sorrow, watching me struggle. Through caring for my family and me, they can work through their feelings and show the love of Christ to one who is struggling. We all need help, and sometimes we need to swallow our pride and accept the love shown to us. In reality, this is a lot easier said than done (especially for us pigheaded men).

CHAPTER 24
NO MORE BUS DRIVING FOR YOU

I hate driving the bus. It is big, traffic around Nashville is awful, and it is not easy to navigate. Monitoring everything, being careful and alert, and just simply driving something that big can be exhausting. As I said, I hate driving the bus – so why am I not happy? She just told me I could no longer drive the bus. I should be doing backflips, but I am not – I am just mad.

About a year before my diagnosis, before my physical condition had fully deteriorated, I sat at the clinic for my medical check-up for my CDL license. Every two years, I went through this process to ensure that it was still safe for me to drive the bus. At that time, I was struggling some, but was still getting by, or so I thought. My medical history told a much different story.

As she looked at my full diagnosis, which did not definitively show Parkinson's yet, and at all the medications I was currently on, she shook her head in silence. "I will be right back," she said. In my head, I thought, "This can't be good." As she came back in, I noticed her holding a stack of papers. She looked at me and said, "I cannot approve your medical card, and you cannot keep driving the bus."

She then said, "If you can get these five doctors to sign off on this, then I will approve your card." I was thinking, "Yeah, right, like my wife will go for this." (She had been after me for years to give this activity up.)

I drove back to school and met with my headmaster at school. When I showed him what the doctor said, he simply said, "Nope, you are not driving anymore." I tried to protest, but he would hear none of it.

As I left that meeting, I will be honest; I was in a foul mood – really, I was ticked. How could they do this to me? I was fine. (Now remember, I did not even like driving the bus.) I was frustrated (my wife was pleased – as were several other people), and I was mad.

Simply put, I was mad that someone else was telling me what I could and could not do. I was 43 years old and still being bossed around. I had the first of many instances over this last year when someone looked at me and said, "No, you cannot do that." As a young man, I did not like this.

I felt like I was losing. It hurt to be told "No," even though I knew it was the right thing to do. I did not want to admit it – my pride did not want to let this go. Little did I know at the time it would be the first of many things that were taken from me. As the year progressed, and my condition worsened, I saw one thing after another that I could not do, or was told I would no longer be doing. It was hard, it hurt, and in some ways, it was humiliating (at least in my mind).

Unless you have experienced this, it is sometimes hard to understand. We do not like to be limited, and just like a child, we often do not want to be told "No." My pride was wounded, and I was hurting. I am still in that process today, discovering what I can and cannot always do, and I wish I could say I was handling it well every time, but it is still hard, and it hurts. I have finally been able to let go of much of the anger, but it is still painful.

Mine's Parkinson's, What's Yours?

In my pride, I do not want to let things go. This process messed with my self-image and forced me to admit and see that I have a struggle, and its name is Parkinson's. I am learning others around me hate this just as much as I do, and in a different way, it is just as hard. Sometimes the hardest things in life, are also the right things. As I have humbled myself, I have begun to be able to see the love that others show when they are telling me, "No." And as much as neither of us wants to say or hear it, we know it is the right thing to do, and it shows a more profound love and commitment than saying "Yes" ever would.

We all have limits, and we all have things we cannot do. We can either choose to focus on those or focus on the good, and what we still can do. Being told no is not the end of the world, and being told "You can't" is not the end of your story. It merely means your story now is going to take a different direction. When someone tells you no (and yes I am preaching to myself), just remember the love and courage it took to say that, because sometimes "No" is the most loving thing that can be said.

CHAPTER 25
WHEN YOUR DREAMS
ARE DYING

What do you want to be when you grow up? What will your family look like? What career will you choose? How many kids will you have? What things will you enjoy doing in your free time? Where are some places you want to travel and visit? Who will you marry? What will you do in retirement? As a young person, and even as you get old, you dream. You imagine what your life will be like, and your hopes and dreams drive you. Yet as I look at my life today, so many dreams are gone, and so many will never happen.

Growing up, and even as an adult, I had dreams, and I saw my future unfolding a certain way. Developing Arthritis at 15 certainly changed some things. I had to give up that fantastic future NBA and NFL career – if you saw me, you would know that is a joke. After developing Arthritis, I thought I had made all the changes and adjustments that I needed. Getting Parkinson's was definitely not part of the plan or the vision I had for my 40's or for my retirement years.

As I sat there, listening to the doctor talk about this disease, it was like watching all the dreams I had vanish. As I read other people's experiences with this disease or information on how it might progress, so many visions for my future evaporated. Everything I had hoped for my future was, in a second, gone.

There were so many things that I already could not do with my family, wife, children, and friends. There were limits I had in my job and ministry. There were so many changes I already had to make, things I already had to give up. Now, even more was being taken from me.

Watching my family struggle through this latest challenge to my health has been hard. I have been forced to watch some of their dreams die. They had visions of what our future would look like, of things we would do. All now seemed changed or destroyed. What this disease was doing and would do to me, to us, in the future, crushed so many visions.

I was not prepared for the grief and sorrow that this would bring. I did not realize how hard it would be to make myself give up so many things I had hoped for. My wife and I dreamed of travel, but how could that happen now – between my health and tight finances, that dream looked like it had vanished. We had planned on retiring together and enjoying life, but now we were meeting with Elder Care Lawyers, and planning for what we would do when or if I landed in a nursing home.

Definitely not the future I planned for or dreamed of. Yet, here we were. This was what our future now looked like. The dreams we had might or might not happen now, so what would our later years look like? So much of what we saw now brought sorrow and doubt. At the very least, we knew that this new road we were on would not be easy.

As these dreams died, what would we do? Would we sink into despair and depression, or would we find new ways to walk forward? As I grieved, I realized that my choice was simple. I could camp out here and let sorrow and bitterness grow at the unfairness of this lot in life my family and I had been given. I could give up on my future and make it impact my life now. Basically, I could sink into despair, or I could keep walking forward, seeking out new dreams.

My life was certainly not turning out as I hoped or wanted. In reality, it was going to get much harder. I had to realize, though, that this disease was not a death sentence. It did not end my life today. Sure, it presented more challenges, and we would definitely have to adjust some things, but it did not mean that everything was gone.

Slowly over time, I realized that just because some dreams had died, it did not mean they were all dead. Just because I might not be able to do some things, did not mean I could do nothing. While I did not know what my future would hold, I knew the One who did, and I also knew the ones walking with me into the future.

So I sit here today, and I realize that my future will not be what I hoped or dreamed. It is not the end. I do not know what tomorrow will look like, but today I will choose whether or not I will give up. Just because some things might not happen as I had hoped, does not mean I have to stop dreaming. All it means is that my dreams will change, and only I can choose if I will stop dreaming or dream again.

All of us, at one point or another, have lost dreams. Things do not turn out as we think or hope they should. When this occurs, we can choose to keep dreaming and face the future with hope, or we can give up and despair about how our life did not turn out as we think it should. Either way, the choice is ours.

Will we dream again? We should, because no one knows what the future holds, and even if the worst happens, that does not mean all the dreams I had are dead. Wherever you find yourself, don't let go of dreams, for those dreams impact and make our future possible. Just because things are hard, that does not mean your future is dead. Sure, they may need adjusting, but dreams, like your future, are fluid and are not set in stone. Who knows what tomorrow will look like – we don't, so don't stop dreaming.

Bright Spots In My Darkness

Now Jesus was telling the disciples a parable to make the point that at all times they ought to pray and not give up and lose heart.

– Luke 18:1

CHAPTER 26
LEARNING TO LIVE
IN THE MOMENT

I have a very eclectic taste in music. If you can think of an era or a genre, I can probably find the song or an artist that I enjoy. Out of all the music, though, my favorite is music from the 50's, 60's, and 70's. There's just something about this music that speaks to my soul. I love it. I have a vast record collection, and my iTunes music library has over 5,000 songs in it. But out of all the music I love, there is no singer I love more than Frankie Valli and the Four Seasons.

The very first record I ever bought was a Four Seasons record ("Walk Like a Man" and "Candy Girl"). The vocals, the songs – everything about them I love, and I have almost every record they ever made. This last year as a birthday present, my teachers gave me a gift certificate to the Nashville Symphony. Now my wife does not quite have the passion for music I have, and she is not always excited about the thought of a trip to the symphony.

Don't get me wrong; she would go if I asked her to, but it would not be her first choice. So, after searching the performance choices, when I announced that Frankie Valli was coming to the symphony and I wanted to go, she casually suggested that I take my son. Now,

Mine's Parkinson's, What's Yours?

you might think what 15-year-old boy would enjoy a concert like this – well, my son would. His music tastes are just as eclectic as mine.

When I told him what we were doing, he was extremely excited. About two weeks after my Parkinson's diagnosis, we attended the concert. The two weeks between my diagnosis and the show had already been filled with difficulties. I had started new medicines which were not working as well, I had passed out in a restaurant (always fun), had my first ambulance ride, and spent the night in the hospital. My Parkinson's journey started off with a bang.

Needless to say, I was battling discouragement and frustration. But tonight was a night that I could lay that all aside, and just spend time with my son. As we sat at the concert, we both had a blast. My son may be the only 15-year-old that knows the words to almost every Four Seasons' song. We sang along, and clapped, and cheered, and had an unbelievable time.

As I sat there watching him, tears filled my eyes a couple of times, as discouragement fought to take over, and I wondered how many more of these memories I would have. How quickly would the disease take me? How many more times would I be able to do something like this with my children?

At that moment, God stopped me and reminded me that I had today. I had this moment, I had this memory – a wonderful memory with my son, sharing music we both loved. And in that moment, I was so thankful. I was grateful for the teachers who gave me this gift. I was thankful for Frankie Valli, still performing at 85 (and being amazing by the way). I was grateful that my son and I could share this love for music.

I realized that it didn't really matter how many more memories I had; what mattered was this moment, and this memory with my son. This is a memory he would never forget. Sometimes we can get lost in what we think might happen in the future, and we forget to cherish the moments that are happening today. Sometimes we can let fear of what might happen, rob us of today.

Will this disease progress? Most likely. Will this disease take things from my family and me? Most definitely. Can it take the experiences we are having right now? Never. Walking out of the concert, I was thankful for today, and I cherished the opportunity to make this memory with my son. Thank you, teachers, for this fantastic gift, and thank you, Frankie Valli, for sharing your gift with us, and helping to create a beautiful memory with my son.

CHAPTER 27
IT'S THE LITTLE THINGS

With chronic illness, there are many dark days. Days that seem bleak and without hope. Days when you can see no light. During *The Hobbit* and *The Lord of the Rings* movies it felt this way. It looked like no matter how hard they fought, they would not succeed, and darkness would envelop them.

In the week after receiving my diagnosis, it seemed as if darkness would overtake me. I had read the stories of so many who had fought this disease, I had looked at the statistics and effects of the disease, and I knew one day it would ultimately win. Add to that my unexpected ambulance ride 4 days after diagnosis for passing out, and darkness seemed poised to choke out what remaining light and hope I had.

That is when it started to happen. Amid my discouragement and me arguing with God, I was thrown a lifeline. I was watching *The Hobbit*, and Gandolf simply reminded others that it is not only the big things that make a difference, but many times it is the small, simple acts of kindness by regular people, that really make a difference, and my family was about to witness this.

As news spread, I began to receive messages. Short texts that simply said, "We love you. We are here for you. Let us know if there is anything we can do for you." Nothing more elaborate than a few, small sentences of caring and support, a small act of kindness. One day, a friend showed up to my house, a Cherry-Coke in hand, and a listening ear, and he simply listened. Another small act of kindness. Cards began to appear in my mailbox, with simple notes of love and encouragement. Again, small acts of love.

There was nothing super elaborate, nothing expensive done, and no considerable expenditure of time. Just small acts of love. There were emails, hospital visits, conversations, and so many little ways that others showed caring. In those small acts of kindness and love, the darkness surrounding me was held at bay.

Sometimes, when others are hurting or struggling, we feel that what we have to give is insignificant, that it is too small to matter. In reality, it is the little reminders of love that shed light into very dark days and give those struggling the courage to keep fighting. Never underestimate what you can do to help someone who is struggling. That small act of kindness may be the only thing holding the darkness at bay in their life, and you might just give them the courage and strength to fight on for another day.

CHAPTER 28
OUR BLIND SPOTS

So many things on my to-do list today. I have dozens of meetings, tasks I need to accomplish, places I need to go, and responsibilities that need my attention. My task list is long, and my day will be even longer. I just don't have time...

How many times have we said the sentence, "I just don't have time to...(fill in the blank)." We are controlled by our calendar, our to-do list, our schedule, and appointments that have been made. We fill every waking minute with things to do, and hold such a tight schedule that even a small deviation "blows everything up." No time for distractions, no time for the unexpected, no time to stop and see what is right before us.

As a father and a school principal, my days are often very full. I have paperwork to complete, observations to conduct, meetings (and meetings and meetings) to attend – and this is just the school side. I have responsibilities at home and to my family, and many days I do not stop for even a second.

As the last year unfolded, things began to change. Before my diagnosis, I did not have any choice but to slow down (because I simply did not have the strength to go non-stop). After my diagnosis, and as the treatments began to take effect, I started to feel better, and my strength and energy returned. Once again, my days quickly began to fill up, and I found myself moving at a breakneck speed through my day.

But even in this, things inside had begun to change. My perspective had definitely shifted, and things that once seemed so crucial and essential were just not as important now. What did I want my focus to be, and where did I want to invest my energy? The reality of a limited amount of time was now very much in the forefront of my mind, and I began to ask myself, what is really important?

As I pondered these questions, I began to have what I can only describe as "God moments" – chance meetings, conversations, introductions, and events. I would run into people I had not seen in years. I met people who were struggling and needed help. I was put into places I never imagined.

I remember one day distinctly. I was out running errands (checking off my to-do list), and I decided to stop into Starbucks for a coffee for my wife (yes, I am always trying to earn brownie points). As I entered, I saw "one of my kids" working. He and I had met just weeks before, to reconnect, and we once again started talking briefly. As we spoke, he motioned to the end of the counter and said, "There is my sister. She would love to see you."

I walked over to her, gave her a hug, and took a seat. For the next hour and a half, we talked, laughed, cried, and encouraged one another. It was not something I had on my agenda, but it was probably the most necessary thing I could do that day. Did it push some things back? Yes. Did it interrupt my plan and schedule? Yes. Was it essential? More than you will ever know.

Before my diagnosis, I missed many opportunities, because I was in a hurry, because my schedule was packed, or because I put priorities on so many other things. Before my diagnosis, I missed many of these God moments, and just a year before, I would have said "Hi", had a brief conversation, and would have missed a blessing to me, and the chance to bless another.

Don't get me wrong; schedules are important, and completing our responsibilities is a must. Yet many times, we are so busy, we miss the opportunities right before us. Right then, the most important place I could be, was that coffee shop, having that conversation. Over the last few months, literally dozens of these "events" have taken place, and each time I have stopped for one, both the other person and I have been blessed and ministered to.

Taking time for these "God moments" is many times that most essential thing we can do. How often are you "too busy" to stop for moments like these? Is your go-to response, "I just don't have time…"? While there will be times when we cannot stop, many times, in reality, we can. I would encourage you to watch for these moments. Look for the opportunities right in front of you to support and minister to others. When you take time for these special moments, not only will you have the opportunity to bless and minister to others, but you will be blessed and ministered to in return. I encourage you to take time and see what is right in front of you. Often, it is the most essential and vital thing you can do.

Learning to Laugh Again

A joyful heart is a good medicine, but a crushed spirit dries up the bones. — Proverbs 17:22

CHAPTER 29
PICKING MY THEME SONG, MY WARPED SENSE OF HUMOR, PART 1

"If one day I have to stop working, maybe I can still get a job at Home Depot doubling as the paint stirring machine?" Every time I repeat that joke, I get a look from people, and in that look, they are not quite sure if they should laugh or be shocked.

Quite honestly, that is the reaction I get from most of my jokes. Very early in our relationship, my wife learned never to be surprised by what came out of my mouth. My jokes are often lame, shocking, out of place, or at the very least, a little offbeat. Having dealt with chronic health issues since the age of 15, and being a young man trapped in an old man's body, I had to learn how to laugh.

How many 15-year-olds use a cane? How many 39-year-olds have had three hip replacements? Almost every doctor visit I went too began with "If you were 60, this would not really surprise me…". If you didn't laugh, you cried (which I did do on occasion). I learned very early that laughter has a healing effect. When you can make light of the situation, it helps to bring things into perspective.

Why then should my Parkinson's diagnosis be any different? Don't get me wrong; there were/are plenty of tears shed, and many tough days, days I want to give up, but I can't live there. So, very quickly after my diagnosis, the jokes began. "Kids, if you want a milkshake, just give me a glass of milk and let me hold it for a little while, or better yet, maybe I can replace the milkshake machine at Chick-fil-A?"

Whenever somebody would ask me to get them a Coke, I would hand it to them with a warning "You may not want to open that for little while, unless you want a soda shower." And when I got someone a drink, I let them know that all of my drinks are shaken, not stirred.

On and on the jokes went, and I found it was a fantastic way, not only to help keep things in perspective, but also to help my children, family, and those around me cope. When a friend asked me, "What's shakin'," I would respond, "Me, but no more than usual." You see, for them, this was just as much of a life sentence. In many ways, they were hurting and just as discouraged as I was. In our darkest hours, laughter reminded us that life will go on and helped us take the next step that we needed to take.

One day my daughter and I were driving in the car, and I said to her, "I need to theme song." "What do you think about 'Shake it Off', by Taylor Swift?" We both laughed and then started thinking of other songs that might fit. Below are some of the ones we came up with:

"Shake it Off", Taylor Swift (Still my daughter's favorite)
"All Shook Up", Elvis Presley
"Shake", Sam Cooke
"Shake, Rattle, and Roll", Bill Hailey & The Comets
"Shake, Shake, Shake, Senora", Harry Belafonte
"Shake Me, Wake Me", Four Tops
"(Shake, Shake, Shake) Shake Your Booty", KC & the Sunshine Band

The list could go on and on. (Which is your favorite?) As we thought of more and more songs, the harder we laughed, and I think it was something we both needed. You see, this is not overwhelming just for me, but also for a 17-year-old, and a 15-year-old, and a young wife (by the way, she did not laugh so much as roll her eyes at my lame sense of humor).

In these simple moments of laughter and silly jokes, it gave us all a peace that we can face this together and make it through. That in spite of sadness, in spite of the challenges, we could still laugh and have joy. It changed our perspective and helped us to see that the mountain was not so gigantic as we thought. It was the exact medicine that we needed. It gave us the strength to take the next step and face whatever was sent our way.

The reality is, each of us, in our own ways, faces difficulties and challenges that seem impossible. It is easy in the midst of these for our joy and laughter to be stolen. In these times, more than any other, we need to find joy and laughter and find something we can laugh about (and someone we can laugh with). We need to be reminded that we will laugh again, because our attitude will significantly affect how we deal with something. I encourage you today, amid your struggle, to find something to laugh about. When you do, that problem may be put into perspective, and the difficulty may not be as insurmountable as it once looked.

CHAPTER 30
MY SUPPORT – MY WARPED SENSE OF HUMOR, PART 2

He stood on my porch, holding a brown paper sack. As he handed it to me, he simply said, "I heard you needed some support." I reached into the bag and pulled out a small box – it was a jockstrap.

It had been a long few days. My sister had just lost her battle with cancer. We had cried more tears than I thought was possible. The day was dark, and our hearts were full of sorrow. When he heard the news, he decided to come over. When I opened that bag, and listened to his comment, and saw the jockstrap, I laughed, and I laughed hard.

It had been so long since I had laughed, and in those moments after my sister's death, I honestly could not see myself smiling again. Pain and sorrow were all I could see, and in that moment, more than a hug, more than some trite words, I needed to laugh. I needed to know that I could laugh again, that life would continue, and that we would get through this. It took a lot of guts for this friend to bring me a jockstrap, but it was exactly what I needed (the laugh that is). I have no doubt that God told this man to bring this to me.

Mine's Parkinson's, What's Yours?

As I began this new journey with Parkinson's, I found that I needed the same thing. In the days and weeks after diagnosis, it was a struggle to see the good. It was easy to get discouraged and frustrated, and I discovered very quickly that I need to face this like I had everything else in life. I needed to find joy and humor in spite of this diagnosis.

I began looking for jokes, memes, and any kind of humor that would help me find my joy and laughter in spite of a very discouraging diagnosis. As I searched, I found a fantastic comedian; one who has struggles as well, but he has found a way to laugh in spite of these circumstances. He is the "Lost Voice Guy" - take time to look him up on YouTube. It is definitely worth it.

This comedian is one of my new heroes. He has reminded me of the truth found in Scripture, "A merry heart does good like a medicine, but a broken spirit dries the bones." (Proverbs 17:22) My ability to walk through the challenges of life is directly related to my attitude on the journey. Scripture talks about the joy of the Lord being my strength. My joy does not come *from* life circumstances but *in spite* of them.

Even in the darkest of moments, I can find joy, and I can find laughter. Every one of us has situations in our life that make it hard to find the joy. We all have events that make us wonder if we will ever laugh again. Yet in these struggles, we can laugh, and we can find joy; sometimes, we may have to look a little harder, but it is there. What support do you need today? What can you laugh about in spite of your challenges? Attitude is everything, and laughter really is good medicine.

Charles E. Mickles Jr.

So Many Questions

But he said to me, "My grace is sufficient for you, for my power is made perfect in weakness." Therefore I will boast all the more gladly about my weakness, so that Christ's power may rest on me. That is why, for Christ's sake, I delight in weakness, in insults, in hardships, in persecutions, in difficulties. For when I am weak, then I am strong. – II Corinthians 12:9-10

CHAPTER 31
CAN HE STILL USE ME?

"You shouldn't be doing that! I will take care of that. Just sit and rest. Let someone else do that! If I find out you did that, you will be in so much trouble. Are you trying to hurt yourself?" Have you ever heard statements like this? I have, and some days it gets very old.

One of the most essential needs of any human is to feel useful. We all want to be needed, and in some ways, we all desire to contribute. This need or feeling is no different for those struggling with chronic illnesses or disabilities. Each of us is born with an innate desire to make a difference.

Very early on in life, due to my arthritis, I struggled with this, because there were just things that I could not do. Out of stubbornness, I would still try to do some of these things, and when I did, I would invariably hear one of those sentences listed above. Often when I heard it, I would become even more determined to do it. My stubbornness and pride would rise up, and I would do what I wanted to anyway. Sometimes it worked out okay – many times, it did not.

In spite of my illness, I took great pride in all that I could do. Over the last few years, though, little by little, things began to change, and not for the better. First, my pain began to increase, forcing me to cut back on the more physical jobs that I did. While frustrating, I somewhat understood. I would still, at times, push myself too far and end up paying for it later (while also hearing a chorus of "I told you so's" from others around me).

But as my Parkinson's progressed, more and more was taken from me. I could no longer drive a bus (and some days even struggled driving a car). I was having more trouble walking and also doing basic tasks. My ability to write and type disappeared. I found it hard to move – things like doing my hair, shaving, buttoning a shirt took forever, and I was beyond exhausted all the time. No longer could I push through, and it was depressing.

I watched my ministry and service in the church begin to disappear. I could no longer do it – the spirit was willing, but the flesh was very weak. I watched my ability to work become more and more difficult. Even completing things around the house was, at times, too much. Everything I had taken pride in was slowly evaporating from my life, and I found myself many days asking, "What good am I? Am I still useful?"

So much of who I was, I realized, was tied up in what I did, and when those things were removed, I no longer saw myself as useful. In these moments, I would cry out to God in frustration, not even sure if He could still use me. Have you ever been in that place, a place in your life when you felt utterly useless? It is a hard place to be in – I know, because many days I was there.

I was so focused on what I could no longer do, that many times I missed the opportunities that I still had. You see, maybe I could not do what I once did, but there were things I could do, even with my physical struggles. Perhaps this was God's way of merely redirecting me and helping me see other ways I could serve and minister to others?

I wish I could say I saw this from the beginning. Still, I am a bit hard-headed and missed some of these "opportunities" along the way because my focus remained on what I could not do. Over time, I began to see that, yes, I was of use and could still make a difference, and once I realized this, a whole new world opened up to me, including starting to write again. I realized that just because I could not serve in some ways, it did not mean that I was no longer useful. It just meant that God could now use me in a different way than He had used me before. As long as I believed I could be useful and make a difference, I could. Only when I decided I was no longer useful, would I cease to be helpful – the decision was entirely mine.

Is it still hard not being able to do some things? Sure it is. However, if I focus on that, I miss so many things I can still do to make a difference, and so many opportunities to be useful and impact others. Yes, I still push myself too much sometimes, and yes, I still hear some of those statements above. When I hear those comments now, though, I don't get quite as discouraged and frustrated (okay, maybe still a little). I realize that these voices are raised in love and concern, and are merely trying to help me see that there are other ways God can continue to use me.

Am I still useful? Yes, as long as I choose to believe I am, and I want to see the opportunities for impact right in front of me. Are you still useful, and can you make an impact? Absolutely, as long as you choose to see the opportunities right in front of you. No matter what your life circumstances look like, we all can impact the world around us. Stop focusing on what you cannot do, and see all you can accomplish. Take time to find your opportunities today.

CHAPTER 32
AM I ENOUGH?

So many things I cannot do. So many ways my body is failing. So many extra things my wife, children, and others have to pick up and do because of my illness. Many decisions must be considered and made because of me and my health issues. I know my wife and children love me, but am I enough?

Every human desires love and relationship. We all need a connection to others because God did not design us to walk through this life alone and in isolation. We were created for relationship and community. That community can take many forms. Sometimes our community is our spouse and children; sometimes that community is family and friends; sometimes that community is work or church. There are so many possible communities out there, and as individuals, we are designed to be part of something.

Chronic illness can be and often is a barrier to this community. It makes relationships much more challenging and brings doubt, confusion, misunderstanding, and pain. It hampers a person's ability to connect with those around them and isolates them in dozens of different ways.

Mine's Parkinson's, What's Yours?

My Parkinson's diagnosis is no different. It affected every avenue of the communities surrounding me. Many times I just would not have the energy to spend times with friends. Sundays would often be a struggle, isolating me from my church family. At home, the pain, exhaustion, and doubt would separate me from my most crucial community – my family. This disease affected every aspect of our relationship, and it caused distance, uncertainty, doubt, and pain.

I would often wonder, especially concerning my family – my wife and my children – would I be enough? As my body failed me, and I could no longer do the things a husband and father should be able to do, would I still be enough? I had seen so many families break up or be destroyed by something like this. When I chased that rabbit of fear down the rabbit hole of the future, I was left with the question, would I or am I enough for my family?

In asking that question, I realized two things. First, I was not giving them the credit they deserved. Second, I was tying their love and relationship to me with one thing – what I could do. I was starting from a false assumption. I reasoned their love and care for me was only because of what I could do, what I could offer, basically, what I brought to the table.

When I evaluated my contribution to these relationships based solely on this, then no, I was not enough. I had to realize though that our relationship was not all about what I could do. Our relationship was much more than that. This was especially hard for me to recognize in my relationship with my wife. I knew she loved me, and I knew she was always there for me, but as my body failed (and would fail even more in the future), fear would grip my heart, and I would ask this question, "Am I enough?"

One night, in particular, we had this hard discussion. It had been a hard week, and we were having to make decisions that should not have to be made by a 44-year-old. I was hurting, I was struggling, and I was battling doubt in so many things. I was frustrated with my situation in life and felt like a failure in so many ways. I felt like and really believed that I could not give her what she needed, and through that prism, the future looked terrifying.

I looked at her. I was heartbroken, thinking of what she was going through with me and would in the future. I hated the pain my illness was causing; I hated the burden she would have to bear; I hated the struggle it added to our relationship, and fear and doubt gripped my heart. I began to listen to the lie in my head that I was not enough. I began to look at so many others walking through struggles and wondered if we would survive – if the pain and struggle would one day become too much.

No matter what I did, I could not shake this feeling. My wife could tell something was wrong, but for weeks I would not share my struggle with her. One day, she finally cornered me and got me to talk, and with tears in my eyes, I simply asked, "Am I enough? I feel like such a burden. I have been given a life sentence and, in many ways, so have you. I can't do the things a husband should do, and it is only going to get worse, and I really wonder if I am enough?" She looked at me and very sweetly said, "Well, that's a stupid question. (If you know my wife, you can probably see her saying that.) Stop asking yourself that; yes, of course you are. Even if I had known all of this, I would still make the same decision."

All these things I focused on, things that were bothering me, shortfalls I had, they were not important to her. She loved me, and she was with me, no matter the course this journey took. While encouraging to hear, I realized that I had to believe it as well, or nothing would change. I had to accept where things were and trust, walking forward in faith. Yes, I might not be able to do so many things, but that did not mean I was not enough. It merely meant things were a little different in my community. I needed to "give myself a break," realize some things were not as important as I thought, and focus on the love and care I was receiving, not what was missing.

Mine's Parkinson's, What's Yours?

Are there still days that are hard and discouraging? Yes. Are there days when I struggle with this question still? Of course. Are there days when I still beat myself up for what I cannot be for those around me? Unfortunately, there are, but those feelings are not from those surrounding me; they are from within. I must continue to battle these lies with the truth that I am loved and that I am enough. Regardless of what I can or cannot do, my worth and my community are not based on that. It is based on a foundation of love, and that makes it, and me, enough.

CHAPTER 33
GOD, I JUST DON'T GET IT

I stand there with someone close to me. We both hug each other through tears that will not stop. Once again, we have been dealt another blow. One more thing to place on the stack of sorrow and discouragement that has been overwhelming the past few years. As we both stand there, trying to get the tears to stop, we are plagued by the simple statement, "God, I just do not get it. I just do not understand."

Maybe you have been in a place like this yourself. You are humming along through life, and things are going okay, and then "WHAM," you are knocked flat. Out of nowhere, you are hit with a problem or struggle. As you slowly get up, and you begin to come to terms with the new normal, you take a small step forward and "whoops" the carpet is pulled out from under you.

You lie there, thinking, "What just happened?" You once again try to get up, and the same thing happens again, and again, and again. Your head is spinning, and you are desperately holding on for dear life, unsure if you can even make it. While I have dealt with some of this my entire life, these last 3 years have been exhausting. Just when we adjusted to one new situation, another would smack us out of nowhere.

Beginning in 2016, that was the story of my life. It started with kidney stones, moved on to a stress fracture in my foot, then another, and then another, all while battling my arthritis, and my undiagnosed Parkinson's. It did not stop there. I developed high blood pressure, a weakened heart function, skin cancer, and sleep apnea, all the while, still struggling with my primary health issues.

When you add to that all the other stuff – family health issues, daily struggles, losses – I started to understand how Job must have felt in chapter one as messenger after messenger after messenger came to share awful news. But today, as I stood there, holding a loved one who was crying, I just kept thinking over and over again, "God, I just don't get it" as I cried with her.

On this day, everything seemed so wrong. How could this be what is supposed to happen? I think we have all been there a time or two, and unfortunately, sometimes, there just are not any answers. Sometimes we are just left saying, I don't get it-this does not make sense, as once again we try to get up from being knocked down.

It is at these times, faith becomes so important. We were never promised an easy or painless life, and unfortunately, life is often full of pain, and at these times, we often do not feel like trusting. I will be honest, the last month has been very hard, and I find myself mentally saying, "I trust you God" over and over again, even when my heart does not feel it. Sometimes faith is choosing to believe, even when your heart is not there. Honestly, many days I am there. I have trusted Him and followed Him for most of my life, and even though so many things have seemed so wrong this year, I choose to keep believing.

This does not make it hurt any less. It does not mean I do not have doubts. It does mean that even in the hard times, I will choose to trust Him, especially when it does not make sense. Many days this is hard, and some days I fail. Even in those times, He is with me, and that is an encouraging thought. What are you walking through right now that does not make sense? I encourage you today, simply begin by stating that you trust Him. Each time I have done this, I eventually find peace, and in my heart and emotions, I can trust Him once again.

CHAPTER 34
HOW WILL MY SUFFERING BE USED

One of the hardest parts about chronic illness is the constant state of being sick. No matter where you turn or what you do, it is the unwelcome passenger tagging along for the ride. Every aspect of life is affected. What you do, how you respond, even what you see is touched by this illness. Often my body feels totally used up, so why would I even consider how I choose to allow this illness to be used?

This really is a very odd question. Several months ago, I was speaking with a pastor friend of mine – a man I deeply respect. Surrounded by students in the school cafeteria, we talked about many things, but specifically my health. The day we were talking happened to be a day I was struggling, quite significantly. Not only was I struggling physically, but emotionally and spiritually; I felt lost. There were so many things overwhelming me at that moment, that it was hard even to talk about.

As we talked, he told me that he was going to send me a sermon that had significantly impacted him. I told him I would listen, and at the time of this writing, I have listened to it at least 4-5 times. As I listened to the speaker, he repeatedly keep emphasizing a point that asked us to consider the purpose of our suffering. What are we allowing God to use our pain for?

As I listened, I realized how much I really was struggling with this idea. My disease was destroying my body, so why would I want it used for something? God, couldn't you use something else in my life? I really do not want to use this for anything. I deeply desire to be rid of this. Why would I want to use something terrible like this for anything?

The message and challenge this man gave genuinely spoke to me and forced me to consider things I had not before. Over the following days, I pondered his question, many times as I walked through our neighborhood for exercise. I know my neighbors think I am a psycho walking through the neighborhood, talking with myself (really, arguing with God). In so many ways, I was tired of being strong. I already had enough object lessons from my health, and I really did not need anything else.

As I considered this message and replayed that question over again, I was reminded of a quote I have known since my youth, "Preach the gospel at all times. When necessary, use words." The quote is attributed to Francis of Assisi, and while there is some debate of whether or not he said this, he did say, "It is no use walking anywhere to preach, unless our walking is our preaching."

With this message and quote, I was reminded that everything in my life either speaks for or against God. Everything I live is sharing, and if I am not living what I am saying, there is a problem. My life circumstances speak volumes about my Lord and my faith.

So now, I was presented with a decision. How will I allow this suffering, this disease, to be used? There were several choices, and none of them would be easy. So, I began each day to ask myself this question. Many things I had done before I now could not, but could that be something He used? Could my pain actually be something good and useful?

And then it happened, as my writing began in earnest, I realized that this is what God had for me at this time. My writing and my daily walk were speaking to others. Through this work, I was showing a picture, example, and message to those surrounding me.

I also began to connect with people through my blog and other Parkinson's websites, and I realized how isolated so many were. Through text, Instant Message, and phone conversations, I was able to connect with people who were walking the same path. People who were struggling and alone, with no one who understood. Most of the time, I did not have answers, and sometimes I did not even have encouragement. Still, each time, I had a listening ear, and I discovered, that is what was needed.

As time marched on, I connected with more and more people battling chronic illness. Doors were also opened for me to speak with others and encourage them out of my suffering. This appeared to be my new ministry – the ministry no one wanted.

So each day I ask myself, "Will I curl up in a ball and give up? Will I let anger and bitterness rule my responses, or allow depression to sideline me, or will I use this to help others?" Whether through a listening ear, encouraging words, laughing with another, supporting, or just giving a hug or shoulder to cry on – how would I allow this struggle to be used by God, not only in my life but also in the lives of others?

This is a choice only each one of us can make, no one can choose this for us. Every day, whether I want to or not, I am letting my struggles and circumstances of life shape the narrative my journey will tell. Either I can permit this sickness to turn me inward, or I can allow God to turn it outward to impact others.

Thankfully, this reminder came at a time when I needed it the most, and this brother reminded me of something I desperately needed to hear and remember. I do not want my suffering to be wasted, so today, I choose to allow Him to use this disease as He sees fit. What will you choose?

I encourage you today, let God use your struggles, not only to help you grow but also to bless another. This does not mean it is easy and that there are no longer hard days. It simply means I have chosen whether or not I will let this disease rule my life.

I am learning that out of my challenges, I have the opportunity to bless others. As I have done this, I have ceased to be a victim of my circumstance. Instead of wallowing in self-pity, I have decided to meet this challenge on my terms. Through this, I have once again found purpose and healing, and you will too.

CHAPTER 35
WHERE ARE YOU GOD?
(WHEN HE IS SILENT)

Today was just another day in what is becoming the new normal for me. Once again, I was greeted with news I did not want. Yet another problem has surfaced, another struggle with my health has been found. This newest challenge will change my life and the life of my family forever. I pray to You, I cry out to You, but instead of answers, more problems seem to pile up. Why aren't You answering me? God, where are You?

So many times in life, but especially over this last year, I have asked this question. I cried out into the darkness, seeking an answer to the simple question, "Why? Why are things so complicated? Why do I have so many health struggles? Why do we seem to go through trial after trial? God, what is going on?

Over and over again, I was greeted with silence, or at least what seemed to be silence. I felt very alone. I did not feel like I was getting any answers, or maybe they were just not the answers I wanted. Was I doing something wrong? Was I not listening? Was He speaking to me, and I was missing it?

I would walk through day after day, struggling to keep moving forward, wondering out loud, "God, where are you?" Overwhelmed with sorrow and struggles, I honestly did not know what to do.

The reality, though, is that God was right there with me. It was not that God was silent, but it was me failing to see that He was right there. Too many times I was equating my struggles with God's absence or me doing something wrong. For surely, if He was there, and I was doing what I should, I would not have these issues.

Other times, I equated my lack of understanding as meaning that God was silent and that He was not speaking to me. I thought that if He was speaking with me, then yes, I would hear and understand.

As I have walked this path this year, I have realized how misguided that thinking is, and how pervasive it is in our Christian culture. Too often, we believe if God is not doing things like we think He should, He must not be with us. We also believe that if we do not understand, He must be absent or not speaking. Sometimes, if we are not protected and delivered from trouble, then He must not be with us.

The reality, though, is that during these times, He is most definitely with us. No matter where we are or the questions we have, He is always with us. Whether we hear Him or not, He is speaking and leading and guiding. Even when we think He is silent, He is there.

One of my favorite stories comes from Europe during the World Wars. "On the wall of a cellar in Cologne, where a number of escaped prisoners of war hid for the duration, there was found this inscription: 'I believe in the sun, even when it is not shining. I believe in love, even when feeling it not. I believe in God even when He is silent'." You see, faith believes, even when we do not understand or cannot see.

I am learning that the question does not need to be "Where is God?" It needs to be, "Where am I?" Often, when I have been in this place, my struggle, my doubts, my fears, and my lack of understanding translated for me into God's absence and silence. Yet over and over in Scripture, we are reminded that He is with us and that He will never leave us or forsake us.

As I walk this steep path, He is walking with me. As I ask Him questions, He hears and answers. In these moments, I must have faith that even if I cannot see or feel Him, He is with me, just as He promised. Even when I think He is silent, He is speaking to me through His Spirit, His Word, and His people, and whether I hear Him or not, I must have faith and trust that He will guide and direct.

When you feel like He is not there or that He is silent, stop, and seek Him. Quiet your heart and mind, and rest in the knowledge and faith that He is with you and that He will never leave you or forsake you. Have confidence that, even in silence, He is with you.

Emotional Up's And Down's

Not that I speak from want, for I have learned to be content in whatever circumstances I am. I know how to get along with humble means, and I also know how to live in prosperity; in any and every circumstance I have learned the secret of being filled and going hungry, both having abundance and suffering need. I can do all things through Him who strengthens me. – Philippians 4:11-13

CHAPTER 36
SOME TEARS ARE NEEDED

It's a typical day, well as normal as my days get. Someone comes up to me and simply asks how I am doing. I start talking, and for no reason I can pinpoint, my eyes well up with tears, and I begin to cry. Embarrassed and frustrated, I simply stop talking, and we stare at each other in silence, neither one sure what to do next.

This scene has played out over and over again during the past months, and really over the previous year. I will merely be talking or doing something ordinary, and I will just be overcome with emotion – sadness, grief, fear. Feelings that, at times, simply overtake me.

Sadness at what my family and I are walking through, and the effects and pain that it causes. Grief over the things I have a lost, and sometimes the death of the future that I saw. Fear of the future and what it will look like. Many times when I started crying, I would look at the person and say, "I don't know why I'm crying."

The reality is, I knew, as did everyone else, exactly why I was in tears. Even though I knew why I was in tears, in my heart, I did not want to admit it. For if I acknowledged it, I would have to admit my weakness, my need, my pain, and my fears, and that would be embarrassing. As a man, and a Christian man at that, I shouldn't be having these feelings. I just need to man up, or simply trust God.

Where did we get such ridiculous ideas that men can't show emotion? That Christians just merrily skip through life on a cloud of denial, pretending that nothing gets to us? Being a man, or being a Christian, does not mean we do not struggle with these things. We have feelings and struggles like everyone else, and there's nothing to be ashamed of or embarrassed by. Sometimes the bravest and most human thing we can do is to show people what's really going on inside. There is nothing wrong with weeping, and nothing wrong with feeling sorrow and grief.

We are not meant to walk through life with the façade that nothing is bothering us, oblivious to the pain and sorrow we are facing. One of my favorite verses of Scripture simply says, "...Weep with those who weep." (Romans 12:15) There will be times when we weep. There will be times when we feel sorrow. To deny that is to deny who we are, and it puts a burden on us we were not meant to bear – that of keeping up appearances.

In life, tears are often the most needed thing. I love the *Lord of the Rings* movies, and Gandolf said it best as he was leaving the Hobbits. He reminded them that some tears are needed, and that is okay. There are going to be events in life that bring tears, and that is not bad.

Sometimes, the best thing we can do for ourselves and those around us is simply to cry and let ourselves feel sorrow and grief, and let those around us simply weep with us. For out of this sorrow, this release, we can find strength to keep moving forward with the community surrounding us. We were not meant to walk through grief alone, and there is nothing wrong or embarrassing with showing tears and letting others see where you really are.

Are my family and I okay? Yes. Are we trusting God? Absolutely. Are we experiencing laughter? Of course. Are we grieving and mourning. Yes. Are tears sometimes shed? Definitely, and that is okay. Occasionally, we just can't hold back the tears, and really, we should not even try. Many times, as we cry, we have ones around us who just simply weep with us, and in doing so, encourage us and give us strength to keep walking.

Charles E. Mickles Jr.

CHAPTER 37
CAN I FORGIVE MYSELF?
(BATTLING GUILT)

I sit there alone, locked in my own thoughts. Silently, I beat myself up for not being the man I think I should be. Daily, I look around, and I see myself (at least in my own mind) letting down those I love – my wife, my children, my family, my friends, even those at work. I am battling so many feelings, and I am so mad at myself for having this disease. I feel so guilty for putting my family through this - has anyone else ever felt this way?

These feelings were so unexpected when I first received my diagnosis of Parkinson's Disease last year. As a 44-year-old man, this is not something I was expecting to deal with and was definitely not in my life's plan. I expected feelings of sadness, anger, depression, but guilt? Why in the world would I feel guilty for developing Parkinson's? I had not done anything to contract this disease, there was nothing I could have done to prevent it, so why in the world would I feel guilty? Even though I could not explain it, it was something I was still feeling.

One morning, I could not sleep (a frequent occurrence with me), so I went downstairs and started flipping around channels on the TV. I noticed a show that seemed interesting, so I decided to stop. Now, I know some of you will probably give me grief for this, but that show was Dr. Phil. Occasionally, I will stop and watch and see how he solves problems and helps others because many times, I find his insights and solutions fascinating.

Thinking back now, I could not even begin to tell you what that episode was about. As I sat there watching, Dr. Phil said one of the most profound things I have heard in a long time, and it was something I desperately needed to hear. He simply told his guest that he needed to forgive himself, that he was not responsible for this, and there is nothing that he could have done about this.

I just sat there, stunned. Tears began to well up in my eyes. "You need to forgive yourself." This phrase kept echoing over and over again in my mind. I could not figure out why this struck me so hard. What do you mean I need to forgive myself? What is there to forgive? Do I need to forgive myself for Parkinson's?

Then it hit me. Much of my struggle with this illness centered around the things I could not do as a husband or father. I felt guilty that my wife and kids were "stuck" with me. I felt guilty for the things I could not do. In this realization, I discovered how upset with myself I was. I was mad at myself for having this disease, and I was upset for not being able to overcome it. I felt guilty that my family had to deal with this, and thought how unfair it was to them.

As these thoughts dawned on me, the truth of Dr. Phil's statement rang true. I was blaming myself for something I had almost no control over. In the process, I was just hurting myself and those around me and isolating myself from others.

Whether it is something we cannot control or mistakes we have made, many times, forgiving ourselves is one of the hardest things to do. We sit there, beating ourselves up for these circumstances, totally unaware of the anger and hurt towards ourselves we feel.

This guilt makes it harder for us to deal with the circumstances and also causes pain and hurt to spill out to those around us. Sometimes, the hardest thing we can do is forgive ourselves. When we forgive ourselves, we can truly begin the process of healing. We can start to move forward and deal with whatever it is that we are facing. Instead of beating ourselves up, we begin the process of healing.

I had to realize that this disease was not my fault. I had to come to terms with the fact that I could do nothing to prevent it. I had to stop feeling guilty for the perceived "burden" I thought I was to my family. I had to let go of the thought that this was unfair to my wife and kids. I had to accept that this is where we are, and I had to forgive myself for having something that I had no control over.

Each of us has something we need to forgive ourselves for in our lives. Many times, we beat ourselves up for things we have done or for things out of our control, but either way, beating ourselves up will not change it. We must have the courage and strength to forgive ourselves and move forward. What is it for you? What are you carrying that you should not be carrying? Let go and forgive yourself and begin the process of healing and moving forward.

CHAPTER 38
A TERRIFYING PROSPECT

I will be honest – I am terrified. As I sit here, I cannot stop thinking about my future, and it consumes me with fear. Being diagnosed with Parkinson's Disease at 44 years of age is not something I ever expected, and has added so much uncertainty in my life. What will my future hold? What will my quality of life be? How are things going to be for my family? Will I still be able to function? Will my family be supported - financially, emotionally? Will this be too much for my wife and kids? Am I a burden? How long can I honestly go on? On and on the questions could go, and as I look at the future, it is a terrifying prospect.

Fear. To some degree, we all battle against it. Often, it presents itself in our lives as worry. There are days when fear, anxiety, and doubt consume our thoughts. We worry about bills, our health, our children, our job, our family, our future, and so many other things. We begin down that road of worry without even realizing it, our thoughts run away with us, and before we know it we are stressed, frazzled, and down the rabbit hole of fear.

Without meaning for it to, fear becomes an overwhelming force in our lives, and colors everything we see and feel. It sometimes becomes all we can see. There are times when this is true of me. No matter how hard I try, I cannot shake this feeling of dread. Today is one of those days for me. My mind is spinning with so many fears, worries, and doubts. It is all-consuming, and today, it is something I am finding very hard to shake.

Like a pit in my stomach, it is a weight I can physically feel in my chest. I try to ignore it, I try to dismiss it, I try to "think positively," but it stays with me, and is still there. It started yesterday with some challenging circumstances. Circumstances that reminded me of how tough this fight really will be. Decisions and events that made me feel like I was already giving up and conceding things to the enemy of Parkinson's. In some ways, I felt like it had already won, and it made me doubt if I was up for this fight and if my family and I would make it.

So many of the questions I listed above have continually swirled through my heart and mind. I have found myself this past year, battling fear and discouragement in a way that I have never fought before. I am fearing for my future, finances, family, relationships, health, and even for my will to keep fighting. I am dreading the unknown.

I have never been one to battle much fear. I have a strong faith that has helped me through so many struggles and a support system that gives me strength and encouragement. As I look to the end, death does not even frighten me, because honestly, in many ways, it will be a release, and I will be at peace. Honestly, at this point, I am more afraid of living and what this life will now look like. Having never really battled fear and worry, this has been a new and unexpected "side-effect" of this disease. I have had faith and support through so many personal struggles and health battles, and yet with this latest battle, very often I find fear consuming me.

I find myself in a daily battle for my heart and mind; a fight that I am struggling to win. Some days I struggle to even have faith. My confidence has been shaken not only in others around me, but also in myself. Sometimes I think, "If this is how I feel now, what in the world will my future look like?" I have never had such a hard time winning a battle, but this one just will not let go. So many days, hour by hour, moment by moment, I am battling this fear and seeking to take these thoughts captive.

Fear, unfortunately, is not something you can wave away with a magic wand. It is not something that you can decide not to feel. It can be very real, especially when looking at a tough and challenging road moving forward. I am often feeling it before I even realize it. So many days, I find myself locked in this battle, a genuine struggle for my heart and mind, one that, at times, I cannot win. It can be easy to "camp out" in this place and let it consume me.

When I find myself here, sometimes, I just get stuck and go further and further down the hole of worry, fear, and doubt. When I am stuck here, I can see no way out, no bright spot, and hope is in very short supply. When I find myself in this place, usually it is because I am trying to battle it on my own. I have locked myself in my thoughts, and like a dog chasing its tail, I can't stop the swirling thoughts, and ultimately, I imagine and fear the worst. This isolation breeds fear and makes it stronger.

Other times, when these feelings begin to grip my heart, people around me step in to strengthen and encourage me by helping me to refocus. They remind me that I am not alone and that I have friends and family standing ready to fight with me and support me. As we talk and I give voice to my fears, I discover that they are not as overwhelming as I initially thought, and I find strength and encouragement to keep fighting.

Because of my deep faith, I sometimes call to remembrance the encouragement found in Scripture:

Deuteronomy 31:8 "He will never leave you nor forsake you. Do not be afraid, do not be discouraged."

Psalm 46:1-2 "God is our refuge and strength, a very present help in trouble. Therefore, we will not fear…".
Psalm 56:3 "When I am afraid, I will trust in you."

My faith reminds me that I am not alone, and I have the One who will strengthen me.

Along with these things, I take time to remember all that I have walked through and overcome – arthritis at 15, emergency stomach surgery, 3 hip replacements/revisions, financial disasters, more medical bills than you can shake a stick at, and more health issues than the geriatrics ward in a nursing home. In this, I am reminded that this is just one more battle, one more mountain to climb, and one more obstacle to overcome. Yes, this might be bigger, it might be harder, and it might ultimately win, but I will choose each day whether to fight it or allow the fear of what "might" happen to tell me to give up.

I wish I could say these things magically take my fear away, but they do not. It is still something very real I feel and battle each day. But, when I am faced with anxiety, I have these things, and it gives me the ability, courage, and strength to decide to take one more step, and the next one, and the one after that. I am discovering that strength and courage is not the absence of fear, but it is choosing to move forward in the face of that fear. It is deciding that I will not be ruled by this fear.

There is much to fear when I look at my uncertain future battling Parkinson's Disease. There is much to fear in decisions I am now having to make. There is much to fear considering how this is affecting my family, finances, relationships, ministry, and health. I do not know what my future holds, or even what tomorrow will look like. I do not know if my worst imaginations will ever come to pass. I have faith, family, friends, so I am not alone. I remember the victories I have had, the things I have overcome, and it gives me strength to fight another day. These things remind me to simply take this disease one day at a time, and trust these things around me so that I can keep moving forward, even in the face of my fears. I may have fears, but each day I will decide if fear has me.

CHAPTER 39
SO ALONE

Hello, my name is Charles, and I am a freak. Not really, but often that is how it felt when telling my story to others - the story of a young man in an 80-year-old body...and now Parkinson's was added to this freak show.

How many people do you know with 3 hip replacements (by age 39)? I know none. How many people had undergone extensive stomach surgery at the age of 17? I know none. How many people were diagnosed with arthritis at 15? I know no one. This list could go on and on. In so many ways, I was different. I was not a typical "guy" and could not do the things that a guy, or a young man, or a husband, or a father, could do.

Don't get me wrong, there is nothing wrong with differences, and in many ways, differences are good and give us strength. But there's a flipside to this. This uniqueness can also be very isolating. When we are different, we can feel very alone. We can feel very out of place.

Often, when those differences are challenges or difficulties, that loneliness is even greater. You can be surrounded by people who love you, care for you, and are great friends and family, and still be

Mine's Parkinson's, What's Yours?

alone. You feel that nobody understands the path you're walking. You look around, and you see nobody like you. People see you, and they're sympathetic, but they genuinely have no idea what you're walking through - at least, that's how it feels.

When I was diagnosed with arthritis at 15, there were no other 15-year-olds in my boat. I received a lot of love, support, and care, but I could not find anybody like me. Recently, I went to a support group for arthritis. I was 43 years old, and by far the youngest person there (by 20+ years) – it was isolating. When I got my diagnosis of Parkinson's, the only people I knew who had Parkinson's were 20 and 30 years older than me. In fact, I discovered that only a small fraction of Parkinson's patients fall in my category of early-onset – and aside from Michael J. Fox, I knew of no one.

It is easy, in these times of loneliness, to lose perspective. I would withdraw and isolate myself even further because no one got it, no one understood (at least that is what I told myself). The further I isolated myself, the more alone I felt – and the cycle kept going and going.

Loneliness can be a battle we all face. It can be brought on by health issues, life events, loss, or any number of things. It can be brought on by differences in how we were created, but whatever the cause, loneliness can be a tough place to be in. It can be discouraging. It can skew our perspective. It can make us think things are worse than they really are. It can make you sad and angry and frustrated, all of which isolate us even further, and cause us to hold people at arm's length.

When I have gotten in these places, sometimes I could get out of them, and sometimes I couldn't. Ultimately, to get out of them, I had to change my perspective. I had to realize, yes, I was different, and yes, others do not know what I'm going through personally. Yes, I'm the only one in this situation. Just because all of these may be true, it does not mean that I'm alone. It may say I'm different, it may mean life is harder, but it does not mean I'm walking through this by myself.

My wife and children do not have to have Parkinson's to know that it's hard and to know that I'm struggling. I don't have to be shot to understand that it hurts. Those around me do not have to have my difficulties to know that it hurts. Sometimes we shortchange those around us by thinking they have to go through what we go through, to love, to care, and to support us.

Sometimes just this simple realization can get us out of the pit. Sometimes we may need medication, a talk with a professional, or just a conversation and hug. Whatever the course, we can get out of this spiral downward, by remembering those around us that love us, and by recognizing that we have a God who will never leave us or forsake us. "Even though I walk through the valley of shadow of death, I will fear no evil, for YOU are with me…" (Psalm 23:4).

Loneliness is often a choice and a perspective that we may have due to the hurt, difficulties, or differences we are facing. Remember, you have a God who loves you and is always with you, and people around you who love and care for you too.

CHAPTER 40
PUT ON A HAPPY FACE – HOW DO I STAY POSITIVE?

"Put on a Happy Face" is one of my favorite songs. I love Dick Van Dyke's version best. It is happy, upbeat, fun, and just makes you feel good. There is only one problem - how do I get to the point of genuinely feeling this, and not merely putting on a happy face/mask? This is a struggle for all dealing with chronic illness. Too often, we simply "put on a happy face," and that is the mask we wear before others.

For me, this has been one of the hardest parts of chronic illness. I am generally an upbeat and positive person anyway, and I HATE feeling sad and depressed. I love to laugh and have fun and usually strive to have an optimistic attitude. Parkinson's, though, has made that hard. Not just because of how I feel daily, but because of what my future most likely will hold.

My future, most likely, is not pretty. Some days, my present is not much better. I struggle with so many things, live in constant pain, battle fatigue, and know that it will not get better, but instead, it will only get worse. How in the world can I be happy, upbeat, and positive facing this disease? How do I feel real happiness and joy, not merely just putting on a smiling face?

I will first admit – this is hard to do. The are many days when I do not personally feel the joy and happiness that I want to have, and for me, that is very hard. There are so many things that rob us of joy in life, even without chronic illness. When you throw that struggle into the mix, sometimes, it feels overwhelming and impossible.

I have struggled with this question many times and even had people ask me how do I remain positive in the face of inevitable hardship. One of the greatest ways to stay positive is getting out of your head. When I sit and think and stew over my current state and the future, I get very discouraged and depressed. It is easy to focus on the pain, and travel down the "What if" road of what might happen. If I do that, there is no chance of being positive.

So instead, I work to take it one day at a time. When I feel myself dwelling on how I feel or what my future holds, I stop and work to focus on something else. Nothing good comes from me dreading or obsessing on what might happen. Sometimes I stop and cry through it and give myself permission to grieve (which is not bad), and then work to redirect my thinking and focus, either on my own or with the help of others.

As I redirect my thinking, I focus on all the blessings I have and all I can be thankful for. Every one of us, no matter how bad we are doing, have blessings and things to be grateful and joyful over. As I consider the blessing I have, it brings me joy and reminds me to keep things in perspective. When I focus on this, I have joy.

Laughter really is a good medicine and learning to laugh about my condition helps. I try not to take myself too seriously, and I have learned to laugh at myself. When I crack jokes about my shaking, or walking, or memory, or balance, or any number of other things, it helps me and others laugh. That laughter helps remove some of the sorrow and seriousness of the illness.

Sometimes, with chronic illness, we feel like we have nothing to offer, but that is such a lie, and so wrong. No matter how bad you are, you have something to offer. Maybe it is a kind word or note, perhaps it is a quiet prayer, maybe it is some type of service, or perhaps it is just a smile, hug, or a listening ear.

When we look beyond our state and help others, it brings purpose and joy. No act of love and care is too small, and it brings joy not just to the receiver, but to the giver also, just as Christ brings joy to my life through His gift. He is my ultimate source of hope and joy, and when focused on Him and His promises, I can have joy in spite of my struggles and future.

As these things are done, the choice to be positive seems natural. Instead of focusing on my future and present condition, through these things, I choose to be positive. Really that is the million-dollar secret I choose. I choose what to focus on, and that choice will dictate my spirit.

Most likely, my future holds pain and deterioration. Currently, there are many issues and struggles associated with this disease that are hard to bear. When focusing on these, joy is almost impossible. When I do the things above, I am encouraged, and it is much easier to be positive, because of what I choose to focus on. Doing these things help me be positive and look at life with hope, and when I do that, joy shows through so that I am not just putting on a happy face.

Charles E. Mickles Jr.

Walking This Journey With Us

So we, though many, are one body in Christ, and are dependent on one another...Love one another with brotherly affection. Outdo one another in showing honor...Be in harmony with one another.
– Romans 12:5, 10, & 16a

CHAPTER 41
BUCKLE UP FOR THE ROLLER COASTER RIDE

A rollercoaster is one of the most accurate descriptions of life. One minute you are chugging along up the hill, and then the bottom drops out, and you are in a freefall. This up and down continues until the ride is over, and often, the same can be said for life.

In so many ways, and in so many aspects of life, this constant up and down is present. One day you're are humming along, and things are going well up on the mountain, the next day the world is turned upside down, and looking around, you have no idea how you got in the valley. With Parkinson's, you never quite know what a day will hold. One day your medicines are working great, and your symptoms are very mild. The next day you get up and you can hardly move, and you really have done nothing different.

These ups and downs are not just physical, many times, they are emotional as well, and often this is tied to how you are doing physically. There are days when I am upbeat and optimistic, and there are days when I am discouraged and I just cannot face it anymore. Days when I am happy and joking, and days when I am in tears and cannot talk about it.

Charles E. Mickles Jr.

Many times, as Christians, we think we should always be up, joyful, and optimistic about the future — that we should always be on the mountain top. But real-life is not like that. In real life, there are serious valleys and days of great discouragement. There are days when we are not okay with our current situation and days that are full of tears.

With Parkinson's, the days are very unpredictable. You will have good days, and you will have bad days — and many times from minute to minute, you will not know which day you will get. On those down days, it is hard to hope, and very hard to see the light. During those valleys, we can beat ourselves up for how we are handling things, causing even more discouragement. In reality, we need to realize that the downtimes are part of life.

We will not always be on the top of the mountain. We will experience valleys. We will have hard days, and these days will cause discouragement. Yesterday, I was laughing and joking, even making jokes about my Parkinson's. Today, I woke up in pain, having only slept three hours, not feeling good at all, and was on the verge of tears many times, and that was okay. It was okay that I was in a valley.

Too often, when we are in the valley, we try to hide it and pretend that we are okay when we are not. By doing that, we do not help ourselves and we rob those around us of the opportunity to support and encourage us. For when we are in the valley, we need our community more than ever. God did not design us to walk always on the mountain. "Yea though I walk through the valley..." — it is right there in Psalm 23 — we will walk through valleys; we will have tough days.

But valleys and tough days are not without hope. As Tauren Wells reminds us, He is the God of the Hills and the Valleys. The rest of that verse in Psalms 23 says, "...I will fear no evil for thou art with me...". On this rollercoaster ride of life, He is with us for every up and down.

Next time you find yourself in a tough day, remember He and your community are with you. Instead of hiding it from them, let them see and welcome their encouragement and help. We all have hard days, and we all need support and assistance. It is not weakness to accept these things – sometimes it is the strongest and most courageous thing you can do.

CHAPTER 42
DRIFTING APART

We sit in a room in silence, side by side, both feeling numb. What is there to say? The hurt and pain of this latest diagnosis, some days, is unbearable. We sit there in uncertainty – will we make it? What does she think of me now? Am I still loveable? Does he even care for me; he seems so distant? It seems like we have not talked in days? How did we get here?

In the months leading up to my diagnosis, many times, the silence was deafening. Things we were so sure of, seemed so uncertain now. We saw the hurt and pain we were each going through, and because of our own hurt, we did not know what to do. Would something we say or do make the other feel worse? What could we do for each other when we were struggling? Often there was nothing that we could do to change things or help.

Each of us was locked in our own private battle, struggling with this set of life circumstances in our own way. She looked at me and saw her husband, the man she loved, slowly slipping away. I looked at her, and saw the burden and pain she was bearing, and saw all I could not do for her. I withdrew even further into myself. Like two ships, passing in the night, we slowly, over time, began to drift apart.

In drifting apart, fear and uncertainty began to take hold. Offenses and insensitivities often imagined or exaggerated stacked up higher and higher, until a wall stood between us. We would sit there, looking at each other, wondering how we got here. At a time when we needed to be pulling together, we seemed to be moving apart, with no idea how to fix it. How did we get here?

This separation was not merely with each other, but also with those around us. Because of the physical struggles and exhaustion, relationships began to fall away. Friends, boys I had mentored, loved ones – seemed so distant, many times because I was too tired to do anything but simply make it through the day.

The separation in these relationships did not happen suddenly, but slowly and unintentionally. The pain, fatigue, hurts, and doubts slowly isolated us from one another, until there was a chasm so deep, there seemed to be no way to bridge it.

Then we got the diagnosis. We loved each other, were there for each other, but still could not bridge the separation. The hurts and loneliness had gone on for so long, it seemed hopeless. My wife put it best, "I miss my best friend." And in that simple statement, the bridge began to be built.

We realized that the separation we felt, was in large part, due to misunderstandings, doubts, hurts, and just our physical circumstances. Slowly these things had caused us to drift apart and stop being intentional with each other. We realized our mindsets had to change.

This story is so familiar to many who battle chronic illness or have experienced significant loss. In our feelings of isolation and pain, we isolate ourselves even further and fulfill what we fear happening. Through many hard conversations and humble apologies, the healing began. We realized that many of the things we thought were just not right. And this was not only with each other but others in our life we had drifted apart from.

Through simple lack of effort and not being intentional, we had lost connection, and in isolation, misunderstood each other and allowed hurt and pain to fill us. Sadly, it took us a while to see this. Still, once we did, we realized how much we loved and needed one another. We intentionally began to build that bridge to once again reconnect with each other.

We realized that all we needed to do was "nothing" for this drifting apart to happen. Whether in our relationship with our spouse, our family, our friends, or our God, this same thing is true. To drift apart, we simply need to do nothing, and when this happens, we eventually look up and wonder, "How did we get here?" As you look at your life, what relationships have you drifted from? Have you been intentional in your relationships? Simple neglect is all it takes. We must be intentional with one another if we desire the relationships to remain healthy and not drift apart.

God sought us out, and we must seek Him. For our relationships to remain healthy, we must do the same thing with each other. I wish I would say this problem was now solved, but it is not, and it is something we must battle against daily. It is never too late to begin building that bridge – don't delay. Be intentional and cross that chasm that is separating you from others. When you do, you may just realize that you were not quite as far apart as you once thought you were.

CHAPTER 43
WE ALL NEED A SAM

As stated in one of my previous chapter, *The Lord of the Rings* movies are some of my favorite. There are so many incredible life lessons and applications tucked away in these fantastic stories. Even though Frodo is tasked with carrying the ring, he has a group around him, supporting him on his journey.

As people are lost, or start to fall away, Frodo makes the decision that he must do this alone. This is his burden only to bear, and he must leave, so others are not hurt. As he paddles away from the shore, Sam calls after him. When Sam can see that Frodo is not returning, he marches into the water, even though he cannot swim.

Sam realizes Frodo cannot do this on his own. As Frodo turns around and pulls Sam into the boat, Sam reminds Frodo that he made a promise, a promise to go with him, and it was a promise he was going to keep.

Even though Frodo was convinced that he could and should make this journey alone, Sam knew better. He knew that Frodo needed him. No matter what the journey threw at them, or even as Frodo changed and lashed out at Sam, he continued to walk with him and help him on his journey.

As I took my first steps along the journey of my battle with Parkinson's, often, I had some of the same thoughts. I would look at this as my journey, my struggle, my fight, and I would try to walk it alone. I would think and sometimes voice to my wife and others, how they would be better off without me. It would be better for them to not take this journey with me because I did not want them to experience the pain and hurt that was coming. I did not want them to bear this burden that I thought was mine alone to carry.

And boy, was I wrong. This journey into the "Mordor" of Parkinson's Disease was not my battle solely to wage. It was a battle that, not just I was facing, but one that my family and friends were battling with me. Whether I wanted them to or not, they were bearing this burden, and they were fighting beside me, sometimes holding me up, in the fight of my life, and nothing would stop them from walking this path with me.

It spite of the hurt and pain I was feeling and spewing onto others, they were still there, walking beside me. It was a picture reminiscent of the promise made to Israel in Deuteronomy 31:6, when they are promised, "..The Lord your God goes with you; He will never leave you or forsake you." Just like the Lord is with me, these "Sams" in my life are here to walk with me, and help and support me along the way.

Sometimes we all make the mistake of thinking we can or need to do something on our own. In reality, we all need a Sam or two. Someone who will walk into the fires of Mordor with us, and fight the battles we are fighting side-by-side. We need someone who, no matter what, is always there, someone who never leaves us.

With Parkinson's, I have learned, I cannot do this alone. I need help, and for someone who does not like to ask for or accept help, this is not an easy thing for me to admit. I need people to walk with me, and I am thankful for people, like my amazing wife, my family, my friends, my coworkers – all my Sams. They are committed to walking this road with me and helping me as I journey into the Mordor of Parkinson's.

What journey are you attempting on your own? Do you have a Sam? Do you have someone who will walk with you and encourage you? Find that Sam. Find that one to walk with you, and even carry you when you cannot go on. Someone who will stay with you until the end. I am thankful to have found those people, and even if you don't have a person now, remember, you always have the Lord, for He will never leave you or forsake you.

CHAPTER 44
MY ONLINE COMMUNITY

I'm so exhausted. No one should have to go through what we are going through. I literally know no one else in person that has this or any of the other crap I have gone through. I feel the same way every single day. I am just ready to quit. I just want to rest. If it were not for Facebook, I would not have anyone in my life that really understands.

We all need community, and we all need to feel that someone understands. The statements above represent just some of the conversations and comments I have seen or written online as I have connected with others around the country and around the world that battle Parkinson's. When I received my diagnosis, I was the only person I knew currently battling Parkinson's. I knew of friends who had family members that fought it, and I knew older people from my past who had it, but no one I knew had this disease, and certainly, no one my age.

When I met with my specialist, I was one of two people, in this practice, that were under 50 dealing with this. As I researched this a little, I discovered that roughly 1,000,000 people in the United States battle Parkinson's. Worldwide, only about 10 million out of 7.53

billion people on the planet have Parkinson's – that's less than ½ of 1% of the population. Out of those, anywhere from 2-5% of those cases are Young Onset Parkinson's Patients, meaning there is only somewhere between 20,000-50,000 instances in the USA (on average, between 400-1,000 per state).

This is not a huge number. Even when I went to the local Young Onset Support Group, I was the youngest one. Realizing this can feel very lonely, many times I wondered if anyone really understood. This was one time I was really thankful for Facebook. As I started looking, I began to find support groups online for not only Parkinson's patients but Young Onset patients. When I found these groups, something amazing was opened up to me.

In messages and posts, I found people putting into words all the things I was feeling. There were times when I or others would vent, and encouragement would come flooding back. There were other times when someone would be struggling with a symptom of this disease, and others would share how they struggled with the same thing and what they did. There was no judgment, no dismissal, no trite phrases thrown around, just community.

It was a community there for one another. A group that truly understood what it felt like. People from all walks of life, backgrounds, ages, beliefs, all around the world, coming together to support and help each other. It was beautiful. It was the first time in my life that with a health struggle I was facing, I genuinely felt understood. This is not to say others around me did not care for me and understand the difficulties I faced, but these people really got it. They lived day in and day out with the same struggle, and in realizing that, there was comfort.

In many ways, it helped to provide hope, encouragement, strength, comfort, laughter, and most importantly, it gave a listening ear. There is something about talking with someone who truly gets it that provides us with strength and comfort. It was a choice that we were all making about how we would walk through this disease. Our decision was to be there for each other. Even if only through a computer screen, we would encourage, strengthen, and sometimes, just give someone a shoulder to cry on.

We all walk through struggles, and many of my online friends have reminded me that I decide how I will walk through this. I can turn inward and think only of myself, or I can reach out and help others out of my own trials. Too often, when we walk through pain, it becomes all about us, but when we walk through pain, we also have another choice and opportunity. We have the opportunity to help others along the way. We can show them that they can still keep going, and that they have people to help them.

What are you walking through right now in your life? Is it something that you feel alone in? Somewhere, someone else is walking the same path you are. Find them, help them, encourage them. Be the shoulder to cry on, and cry on their shoulder. Laugh with them; encourage them. Let them know you get it and find someone that understands where you are. We all have the opportunity to comfort others with the comfort we receive. We just simply must choose to give and receive from a community that understands and is walking the same path.

I am very thankful for the friends I have already met that are walking this path. I hate that they are walking through this pain. Still, I am grateful that I have found this "tribe" to walk with me on this new journey of life. I am thankful for those that have taken the time to talk with me and encourage me out of their struggle, for they truly do understand. Out of their own pain and struggle, they have helped another, and in this, shown genuine love for others.

CHAPTER 45
SILENCE CAN BE GOLDEN

Life can really knock you around some days. Sometimes while you are still reeling from the first punch, a 2nd, 3rd, or 4th one comes right behind it. You can't even catch your breath, let alone get back on your feet before you are knocked down again, and just when you think it can get no worse, you get "encouraged" by someone who really should learn the art of silence.

Christians, and not just Christians, but people in general, say dumb things. Often these things have not been thought out before they come out, and they end up doing more damage than good. After my sister passed away, I cannot tell you how many people told me, "God has a plan" or quoted a verse to me about trusting Him. There is nothing wrong with speaking these things, in fact, we should encourage one another with His Word, but timing is everything.

After about the 50th time hearing this, I told my wife, "If one more person tells me God has a plan, I am going to punch them." (Don't worry, I did not punch anyone.) While I was speaking a little tongue-in-cheek, it was frustrating. In my head, I knew God had a plan, but God and I at the moment were debating whether or not that plan stunk (which I thought it did).

I was hurting, doubting, angry, and heavy-hearted. I was not responding in the most Christian manner to this struggle, and I did not need to be reminded that I was not. When I heard this or something like this, I was reminded that I was not trusting God at that moment and that I was not responding as a Christian should.

When I got my Parkinson's diagnosis, I felt many of the same things, but this time, I was reminded again and again, "It could be worse." Really, I thought, because this really stinks, and the future is not really bright, and the best you got for me is ,"It could be worse." Yes, they were correct, it could be worse, but this was pretty bad, and there were not many bright spots. I was struggling emotionally, spiritually, and relationally. God and I were having serious arguments about the ridiculousness of yet another health problem. "It could be worse" sounded much more like "suck it up" in those first few days.

Since, I have heard many, many more comments, that if thought out, probably would not have been said. I have been told that I look fine, that my struggle is just physical, not emotional, that I should be thankful that it is not cancer (which I have dealt with) – on and on the list could go. I know that most people would not understand (and I pray they never do), how throwaway comments not thoroughly thought out can make someone at times with a chronic illness feel.

Today, months later, I would agree with some of these statements (except the physical not emotional comment). Still, during those first few weeks, I was just not there. Often people are uncomfortable with suffering, and we want to find that "magic bullet" that will encourage and fix the problem. We want to fix things for those we care about, but sometimes we can't. We never stop to think about how it will sound or make the person feel. In the process of seeking to support, we end up doing more damage.

Frankie Valli and the Four Seasons once sang "Silence is Golden," and that may be one of the most helpful statements in the English language. You see, sometimes, there is nothing to say, and there are no words that will fix the problem. Some of the most encouraging moments after my diagnosis came in the form of a simple and silent hug. Sometimes the person would look at me a say, "I don't know what to say" or would simply state, "this sucks (pardon the language)" and then give me a hug.

They knew that sometimes there is nothing you can say. There is no magic phrase that will fix everything and take away the pain. They were just there to love me and sometimes, just sit and cry with me. These people had also walked through some severe struggles and had received these "words of encouragement." They understood that at that moment I just needed to be loved and cared for, and that often came in silence.

Yes, we should encourage one another and help them remain grounded during storms, but we must be sure that what we are saying is helpful, and the Spirit can help us if we let Him lead. Next time someone is struggling, just give them a hug, sit with them in silence, or be present in their life, and be okay with not offering some great nugget of faith or religion. Meet them where they are and grieve with them. Let them know they are loved, and you are there to support them. It will mean more to them than anything you could ever say. Silence, indeed, can be golden.

CHAPTER 46
WHAT'S WRONG WITH YOU

She called over and asked if she could see me. As she entered my office, she asked if she could close the door. After the door was shut, she looked at me and simply asked, "What's your problem? Are you alright?" I stood there, not sure how to answer because I was anything but alright.

It had been a very rough year physically. Unknown to me at the time, I was in the early days of my battle with Parkinson's Disease. In addition to that, I was in extreme pain constantly. My arthritis had flared up again, I was having to use a cane many days, my knees were the size of cantaloupes, and I was having them drained almost bi-weekly. Each day was a struggle, and I was a few months away from yet another hip replacement. Needless to say, it was rough.

A dear friend and co-worker came to my office and said those exact words, "What is wrong with you? Are you okay? You are walking around snapping at people, and you seem so unhappy and upset. I see how you are reacting to others, and that is just not you. What is going on?"

Mine's Parkinson's, What's Yours?

At first, when I heard this, I was upset and a little annoyed. "How dare she talk to me like this? What business is it of hers? I'm not snapping at people. Doesn't she know the pain I am in every day?" Uncharacteristically for me, I held my tongue and realized how concerned she really was for me. As I thought about what she said, I began to see that she was right.

In my pain and struggle, I was "bleeding out" on all of those around me. I was letting my frustration with my current circumstances affect how I treated and interacted with those around me. I was responding in frustration, but not because of something they had done, but because I was in pain, and I was tired.

The courage this took to confront me, is something I admire and am truly so thankful for, because, I was missing what I was doing. I did not see how my pain and exhaustion was affecting others around me by how I was responding to them.

This year, I have had to battle some of the same feelings, pain, and exhaustion. This time it was my wife, who courageously looked at me one day, and just simply said, "Each day I brace myself because I do not know who I am coming home to. Is it the happy Ched who is ok with things that day, or is it the frustrated and angry Ched lashing out at everyone around him?"

And she was right, I was all over the place emotionally. Some might say it is understandable given all I am walking through, but the reality is, it is not. In my frustration with this disease, I found myself once again lashing out at those closest to me. I was hurting those around me because of the pain I was feeling. I was tired and hurting and so discouraged. Once again, I did not even see it. She was not mad or upset, but she was worried because this was not me. This was not the person I usually was. She realized it was my pain and hurt coming out, and she wanted to help me.

Often, our pain colors so many things in our lives. It can spill out in ways we could never imagine. As I listened to my wife, I knew some things had to change. I realized that I could not let my current state of hurt be taken out on all of those around me. I realized I needed to deal with these feelings of anger and frustration.

Now, this does not mean I am never down or upset, or that I now never hurt those around me. It does mean, I have begun to work through these feelings with the help of others. I do not want to hurt those around me or respond out of my anger or pain.

As I talk with other people, I realize that this is not exclusive to me. We all have this problem at times. In frustration, annoyance, anger, or pain, we respond in ways we usually never would, simply because we are struggling. We lash out, not intending to, but actually hurting those we love. We let our feelings and our current state dictate our actions.

While not perfect, this is something I am trying to be more conscious of in my dealings with others. As I rest in Him, and follow the Spirit, not only am I dealing with the pain, but hopefully, I am letting Him guide my heart and reactions. Proverbs 18:21 reminds us that the tongue holds the power of death and life. By my reactions and interactions with others, I decide which I am going to give.

How has your struggle affected your dealings with others? Does someone need to ask you, "What's wrong with you?" As you look at your day, are you breathing life or death into others? As frustrating and painful as life can sometimes be, and as hard as our struggles get, we have the choice to respond out of our struggle with either hurt or life. This is a moment by moment choice. Which response will you choose?

CHAPTER 47
IN SICKNESS AND
IN HEALTH

I promise to love you and comfort you,
To honor and keep you,
For better or worse,
For richer or poorer,
In sickness and in health,
So long as we both shall live…

If you have ever been to a wedding ceremony, you have heard some version of these vows. Vows that two make for a lifetime. No matter what occurs, no matter how good or bad it is, a commitment is made to be there for each other. It is a blind commitment, made with no knowledge of the future. It is a promise to be there for and support each other in the best of times and the worst of times.

Recently, I had the opportunity to attend the wedding of a young lady who used to be one of my students. Her father was also one of my teachers (one of my favorite and most influential teachers), and we have known and been part of their family for years. I sat there watching the beautiful young couple take their first steps into a future that would be their life together as husband and wife.

I sat there with my arm around my bride (partly because it was so cold). I listened as they recited these vows affirming their life-long commitment, I was taken back to a day very similar, 22 years ago. It was a cold, wintery day, but a day full of love and warmth as my wife and I stood together and shared some of these same words as we committed to a life with each other.

As a young couple, we had no idea the path our lives would take, and what the future held in store for us. There have been so many good and beautiful days – the births of our children, wonderful trips, loving, quiet evenings – and so many more. But, there have also been some sad and difficult days – health issues, death, family struggles – days that have tested us in ways we could never have imagined.

This year has held many of the latter days. Days that were unbelievably hard. Days when we were not sure what to do. When I received word that I had Parkinson's Disease, in many ways, our world stopped. We had no idea what to do next, or even what our future would look like. In sickness…that is what we had said, but this was the latest in a long string of "sicknesses." What about the health part – when did we get that part?

In the months that followed, I would sit there looking at my wife, feeling sorry for what she had gotten herself into. I felt like she had received a raw deal, and many times I wondered if she regretted her choice and if she would do the same thing all over again knowing what she knew now. Yes, she knew I had health issues, but this was a game-changer. It was something that would consume our lives, and slowly over time, take the man she loved. I hurt for her because it just was not fair. She did not deserve to bear this burden. This was not what she had signed up for.

As I sat there, listening to this young couple make this promise to each other, I was gently reminded that my perspective was off. You see, this is precisely what she had signed up for. We had given each other a blank check and promised that no matter what we walked through, we would be there for each other. No, the hand we were dealt was not fair, and yes, it would be hard. There would be days when we wanted to give up, and days that were painful.

As I watched this young couple starting out on this journey, I looked over at my wife and was thankful that not only had she made this promise, but in the face of awful news, she had decided to stick with me in sickness. Our marriage has been overshadowed by illness for most of the 22 years, and yet, our commitment is strong.

We are early on this journey, but we have weathered so much already in these last two decades. Do I know what the future holds – no. I have no idea what will happen or how bad things will get. One thing I do know – I know the person who gave me that blank check. I know the love and care for me she has shown already. I know what she has already walked through with me. I know the love and commitment she has for me.

This will not be an easy path. It is not fair that my wife has to walk this with me. There will be days when we frustrate and anger each other. Days when we cry and want to give up. Days when fear overwhelms us. But there will also be days of joy and love, and days that are good. In each of those days, we will have a choice whether or not to fulfill this commitment. As I watched this young couple, I was reminded of the promise we made to each other, the promise she made to me. I was overwhelmed with thankfulness, and I was grateful that this young couple had reminded me of something I so desperately needed to be reminded of.

Even though I struggle knowing that she will have to deal with more sickness than health, more worse and less better, I know her heart, and I know our love. I know that she is here for me and that she does not regret her choice. In sickness and in worse, we are here for each other because of our love, and that would help us weather this latest storm. Happy Anniversary, my love – thank you for 22 years. Here's hoping for 22 more.

Charles E. Mickles Jr.

What I Am Learning

So teach us to number our days that we may get a heart of wisdom.
— Psalm 90:12

CHAPTER 48
...BUT GOD (THERE IS ALWAYS HOPE)

"You intended to harm me, but God intended it for good..."
Genesis 50:20

Joseph's brothers stood before him, terrified. He was now the second most powerful man in the world. This was the boy they had tormented, thrown into a pit, sold into slavery – this was the man that now stood before them. He now held their fate in his hand, just as they had held his.

What would he do? Would he finally have his revenge? Would he torture them, kill them, or simply sell them into slavery? How would this end – what would their fate be?

As Joseph stood before them, he understood something that they did not. When he had been sold into slavery, when he was successful as a servant, when he was falsely accused, thrown into prison, then let out of jail and elevated to second in command of Egypt – in each and every situation, in the good and the bad – God was with him.

Joseph understood that there were difficulties in life, **_but God_** was with him and had a plan. This is something that I had to remember as I began this new journey in life. Joseph understood that the event was not the destination, it was not the period at the end of the sentence, but merely a comma, a slight pause, before He finished the story.

This is something that I had to realize. My diagnosis was not the end of my story. My struggle did not mean it was over. It merely said that God's power and grace and mercy could all the more shine through my life.

I have Parkinson's disease, but God…
I have arthritis, but God…
I have lost family members, but God…
I have struggled with depression, but God…
I have had three hip replacements, but God…
I am worried about the future, but God…
I am always in pain, but God…

You see, **_But God_** changes the statement entirely. Instead of finality, it bestows hope. It reminds us that our current struggle is not the end. It reminds us that while this situation seems dark, there is one there to help us and strengthen us. He's there to walk with us and provide us hope, even when there seems to be none.

If you read the story of Joseph, every time there's a struggle, Genesis reminds us, "…and the Lord was with Joseph." Joseph understood that God was with him in the good and the bad. He realized that while struggles were hard, God was with Him. And through his struggles, he was able to bless others.

As I walk this new challenge in life, I must remember the same thing. I have Parkinson's disease, but God strengthens me. I am discouraged, but God gives me hope. I am sad about this latest struggle, but God gives me compassion and joy. I am tired, but God gives me rest.

Mine's Parkinson's, What's Yours?

What is your "but God" struggle? In what situation of your life do you need to remember this? Each and every day, in every circumstance, I have the choice of where to live. I can live in my circumstances, or I can remember "but God" and live in the hope that these two words bring.

Yet this I call to mind
    and therefore I have hope:
Because of the Lord's great love we are not consumed,
    for his compassions never fail.
They are new every morning;
    great is your faithfulness.
I say to myself, "The Lord is my portion;
    therefore I will wait for him."
-Lamentations 3:21-24

Remember, no matter how dark or hard the struggle is, He is with you, and He will walk with you. I may feel overwhelmed and alone, but God is with me always, and this simple remembrance brings me Hope.

CHAPTER 49
AS ELVIS WOULD SAY, "I'M ALL SHOOK UP!"

"I'm Fine." How many times a day do we say this or hear this from others? It is our go-to response to the question, "How are you doing?" We give this response without even thinking, and often, when often we are anything but fine. Why do we have such a hard time being honest?

I will admit, this PERFECTLY describes me. I have had physical difficulties for so long that saying "I'm fine" simply became a habit. I spent every day in pain. Almost every action was a struggle. I was always tired, and I see-sawed between happiness and discouragement. Often, I just did not want to talk about it, because I was tired of discussing and hearing about it.

So, it was just easier to say fine, smile, and have everyone move on with their day. I rationalized this little white lie by simply telling myself that they did not really want to know anyway. What we both wanted, I told myself, was a quick, simple interaction so that we could both get on with our day, having at least been pleasant to each other.

While this was true sometimes, at other times, I just did not want others to know I was struggling. I felt better keeping the mask up and the illusion of having everything together and in-tact. For me, it was a matter of pride, to show others how well I could handle things. It was also a matter of fear – I did not want to appear vulnerable or weak to anyone.

In reality, those who knew me best were not fooled, and some really close to me called me on it more than once. I will admit, when I got my diagnosis of Parkinson's, both literally and figuratively, I was "All Shook Up" – pun intended. When my symptoms got worse, it was the first time in my life that I could not just push on through. I could not merely "put on a happy face" and muscle through, mainly because I felt so bad. Once I had the diagnosis, sometimes I could not even talk about it without tears; they would just flow no matter what I did.

In those moments, I could not even fake being okay, and I discovered how much I had shortchanged myself and others. By not sharing with people where I really was or how I was doing, I was robbing myself and others. I was depriving myself of the simple release of my feelings and of the comfort from others that sharing brought. I was robbing others of the chance to care and support, and I was taking from us both the opportunity to grow stronger in our relationship.

It is not easy for any of us to be vulnerable and share with others if we are struggling, but it is necessary in so many ways. Without letting others know where we really are, we will never find the strength, healing, encouragement, and support we need to move forward. Instead, we will isolate ourselves and fall into discouragement and depression.

The next time you ask someone, "How are you?", make sure you are ready for any answer, and if you are asked that question, make sure you give an honest answer. If we never let people know how we are genuinely doing, how will we ever find the strength, healing, and comfort we need to keep moving forward. We need to put down the masks and be honest with where we really are – and yes, this is the pot calling the kettle black.

So, how am I doing? Both emotionally and physically, literally and metaphorically, I'm all shook up (that's a joke, but also very accurate). Honestly, though, there have been good days and sad days. Days when I could laugh, and days when I just cried. Days I felt upbeat, and days of immense discouragement. Days when nothing could stop me and days when I did not think I could go on. Today is a good day, I'm tired, but encouraged, because I know He is with me. We will see how tomorrow goes, but if you ask, I promise I will be honest.

CHAPTER 50
IT IS BETTER WITH MY SOUL

Though Satan should buffet,
Though trials should come,
Let this blessed assurance control,
That Christ has regarded my helpless estate,
And has shed His own Blood for my soul.
- *It Is Well With My Soul*

What a ride this year has been! I can only think of one previous year, the year we lost my sister when our family has been buffeted and tossed as much as we have this year. It has been a year of hardship and sorrow and many discouraging days.

In a previous chapter, I wrote, "It is not well with my soul", and that is precisely how I felt. I totally identified in my heart and mind with the lines from the song, "...When sorrows like sea billows roll...though Satan should buffet, though trials should come..." Even though He had taught me to say, I could not bring myself to say, "It is well with my soul."

Everything inside of me was screaming the opposite. As trial after trial after trial hit our family, and sorrow and loss piled high, nothing seemed "well" in our lives. So much happened this year, it has almost left my family and I numb. Processing these struggles seemed impossible because no sooner was one thing over than another started. People started jokingly referring to me as "Job."

Through the days of struggle and despair, we tried to keep going, but most days, it was not well. In fact, as I write this, I am sitting in the hospital on Christmas Eve, helping my wife as she recovers from knee replacement surgery. Hey, I can't have all the fun. And with this event, the year comes to a close with a bang, just as it began. In many ways, the perfect bookend to a rather unbelievable and challenging year.

Yet as I sit here today, while I may not be able always to say, "It is well with my soul", I can honestly say it is "better" with my soul. Six months ago, I was not even sure I would get back to this place. So much doubt overshadowed my life. Frustration, anger, and sadness seemed to be my constant companions.

So overwhelmed with my fate, and struggling to trust God, more and more things piled on, culminating in this hospital stay. I finally got to the point where I would just laugh because the stories were just too much to believe. God and I had some interesting conversations regarding His plan and warped sense of humor. In spite of all of this, God continued to walk with us. We were surrounded by so many who helped hold us during these challenging days as we tried to navigate this new norm.

As I talked with God, and honestly shared with Him and others where I was, I noticed that healing slowly began. Everything was not all of a sudden "coming up roses" (clearly since I am writing this from a hospital, LOL). Still, as we took things one day at a time, we realized that He and others were with us, and He would provide.

Was it still hard – Yes! Were there days full of sorrow – absolutely! Did we still have doubts and frustrations – of course. But God was beginning to heal, and we were learning that He would see us through. We have been shown love and cared for in hundreds of ways. I have counseled with others, and also found that God still had things for me to do. As a family, we are beginning to learn that sometimes, just being okay is okay, and just taking that next step in faith allows you to take the one after that.

So today, it is "better" with my soul. It does not mean that we won't have bad days, and it does not mean that there will be no more good days, but as we take things one day at a time, we are seeing Him in little ways. We are finding our footing and learning that we can get back to the place that it is well with our souls, because through it all, He is here.

This hymn was written out of great tragedy. The sorrow for the author was overwhelming. In his struggle, he was reminded of the goodness and love of God. Each of us needs to be reminded of this truth, even at times when we do not feel it. This continues to be a journey for me, and one that I see many people walking. I pray that God blesses you, and in spite of your circumstances, gets you back to the place where it is well, or at least better, with your soul.

CHAPTER 51
SOME DAYS I JUST NEED TO COUNT MY BLESSINGS

One of my absolute favorite movies of all time (besides Star Wars) has to be *White Christmas*. I love the story, the settings, the actors, the choreography, but most of all, I love the music. The songs, in my opinion, are some of the best, and when I hear them, instantly, I think "Christmas."

In this movie, there is one song that touches me like no other. This is a song I have heard hundreds of times, and no matter how often I listen to it, I never get tired of it. Late one night, Bing Crosby and Rosemary Clooney can't sleep. They meet in the lodge, sit by the fireplace, and begin singing a simple, yet powerful song about counting your blessings.

It is easy when you are battling chronic illness, or really facing any problem, for it to consume your focus. Because it is always there, or sometimes because of the constant pain or struggle, or even sometimes because the heartache is so deep, it can become tough to see past it. It literally becomes all you can see and becomes the focus of your life.

Mine's Parkinson's, What's Yours?

When this happens, all other things are crowded out. Everything is viewed through this event or condition, and it colors everything you see. This problem, this difficulty crowds from view all the truly beautiful things in life.

Instead of seeing the blessings and joys, we see the problems and hurt. When this happens, we miss many things, and fail to see that in spite of this challenge, we are blessed. In my almost 30 years of battling chronic illness and pain, and especially with my latest diagnosis of Parkinson's, there have been days when this has been very hard to see.

Many days, I have succumbed to discouragement and depression because all I could see was the pain and the future that most likely waited for me. When this became my focus, all other things were blocked from my vision, and my discouragement only grew deeper.

It is during these times, when I need others around me to help me see how truly blessed I am:

I have an amazing wife and children.
I love my job (and I can still do it at this point) – nothing beats spending the day with kids!!!
I have great friends walking with me.
I have great coworkers, teachers, that I get to spend every day with.
I have a fantastic family (over 50 of us) that love and support each other.
I can still help provide for my family.
I can do things to help provide for my family's future needs.
I have an amazing church family to encourage us.

On and on, the list could go. As I view it, I am reminded that in spite of the pain, diagnosis, or the future, I am a blessed man. This thought does not take away the pain and difficulty, but it helps to put it in perspective and remind me that no matter the problems I face, there are still many, many blessings for which I can be thankful.

What is your list of blessings? No matter how bad things are – and things have been pretty bad at different points in my journey – there are always blessings present in life. Which are you counting, your problems, or your blessings? I encourage you today, take time, and remember all the things that are blessings in your life. When you count them instead of counting and focusing on your struggles, you may find you have more blessings than you realized. When faced with worry and discouragement, there is no greater cure than simply remembering the blessings in your life. Take time today to count just some of those blessings – it may just change your focus and help you see life from a slightly different perspective.

CHAPTER 52
I AM NOT THANKFUL
FOR PARKINSON'S

'Tis the season. It is the time of year (if you can get past all the Christmas stuff already out) that we take time to be thankful. It is a time of year when we remember and give thanks for all we have, but this year, there is one thing I am not grateful for, and I am not sure I ever will be. I must admit, I am just not thankful for Parkinson's.

I know, it's kind of ironic that a chapter written during the "Thankful" season of Thanksgiving would start off with something I am not thankful for. Don't get me wrong, I have lots to be thankful for: a wonderful, loving wife, two amazing children, a supportive and amazing family, a home, funds to pay bills, a great job, ministry, and so much more. This list is just the tip of the iceberg. I could fill a page with hundreds of things I could be thankful for, but I just cannot bring myself to be thankful for Parkinson's or my other chronic illnesses.

How can you be thankful for something that causes so much pain, discouragement, frustration, and so much uncertainty for the future. I have had to make awful decisions in the face of this disease, and I have watched my family walk through pain and discouragement, and

I am unable to fix it for them. How in the world could I be thankful for this?

As hard as this year has been, and as unthankful as I am for Parkinson's, I do have many things from this past year that I can be thankful for. I am grateful that this last year, I have begun once again to see what is truly important. So often we get so caught up in insignificant things that we lose sight of that which is most important. This year I have been reminded of what really is important in life.

This last year, I have had to let go of many frustrations and aggravations, and realized they are not worth my time and energy. Some things that would upset me and frustrate me are now just not worth getting worked up over.

During the past several months, I have realized how unintentional I can sometimes be in life. I have not taken time for the things I should, and not been intentional in how I lived and interacted with others. I have not made time for what is most important, and I am seeing that this type of attitude cannot continue.

I have also seen that in some ways, my focus is not where it should have been. It is easy to lose focus or focus on the less important things, and miss what is truly important and what needs our attention.

I have been reminded this year that I have limited time to impact others. I have had to ask myself what I am doing with this most recent life circumstance? This thought has helped me re-evaluate and refocus on what I really need to spend time on.

This year has reminded me how important family and friends really are. The love, care, and support we give to one another cannot be understated. It is something that many times we take for granted, and something that we often let small things get in the way of, but showing each other this love and support is so very important.

I also have been reminded how petty, and small so many offenses are. We get worked up over things that really are not important.

Instead of forgiveness, we carry anger, hurt, and even bitterness, and allow it to separate us from those we love. With such limited time on earth, we really do not have time for this.

This list represents just some of the things I have learned this year, and as hard as it is to admit this, I am not sure I would have seen them without my most recent health challenge. This diagnosis has shown or reminded me of things I needed to see. Don't get me wrong, I hate this disease, but some things in me have changed as a result of this illness.

I am not, and probably will not ever be, thankful for Parkinson's Disease, but I am grateful for what it has shown me and reminded me of. For through these reminders, I am once again seeing what indeed is essential. So, as I said above, I am not thankful for Parkinson's. Still, I am grateful for the things I have been reminded of this year, and I am thankful for the new perspective it has given me in so many areas. I pray that each of us, in spite of our challenges, can find things to give thanks for.

CHAPTER 53
IT'S YOU I LIKE

As a child, he walked into my living room each day and asked the simple question, "Won't you be my neighbor?" With his cardigan sweaters, sneakers, and simple, quiet ways, he took millions of children and me down many paths of discovery. He taught us beautiful lessons in his quiet way. Each and every day, he reminded me that I was special just the way I was, and this simple lesson is something I need to remember every single day.

It was a simple song. No complicated lyrics. No huge orchestra. Just a quiet voice and a simple piano melody that reminded us that each person was special. Mr. Rogers told us each day, in that beautiful song, "It's you I like".

"It's you I like," such a simple message, a quiet reminder, that I was special just as I was. As a child, I will be honest, I did not always understand the importance of this statement. I did not always realize the power and significance of this fantastic gift. In one sentence, I was told that I was not a mistake, but that I was unique and significant, and that I had a purpose.

Mine's Parkinson's, What's Yours?

As I grew older, I carried this message with me. I was reminded often of these words, not just by Mr. Rogers, but by my parents, who told me over and over that God had a unique purpose for my life. From the first days I began battling Chronic Illness in the form of crippling Arthritis, I remembered these words. I knew that in spite of my challenges and differences, I was created special, and I was loved.

When faced with this latest diagnosis of Parkinson's Disease, though, this was something I began to doubt. Self-assurance gone, uncertainty in my future, the pain of daily living all filled my mind. The doubt I faced because of the burden I perceived myself to be crowded this vital message out of my mind. All of these things combined and overtook my thinking, and in those moments, I would question how anyone could say I was special. Some days I did not see myself as unique, but as someone who was trapped in a broken body – what was special about that?

Mr. Rogers has always been a hero of mine and someone I tried to pattern my life after. It is ironic at a time when I was struggling, the love many had for this man was rekindled, and there was a revival of his simple lessons that he shared with us each day. This week, as the release of his new movie drew near, I was driving home, and heard a song I had not heard in a while. It was the song I referenced above, and in that simple song, I was reminded of those lessons I had learned so long ago.

In a time when I was battling self-doubt and uncertainty and when I was questioning how I could be loved, this man reminded me that it was me he liked and that there were many more that felt this way. Battling the daily pain, exhaustion, and the struggle of chronic illness wears on a person in so many ways. It causes one to doubt themselves and doubt those around them because of the burden they perceive themselves to be. Even though this is not accurate or true, to the person in the struggle, nothing seems more real.

Each day is a battle to see the truth and brings new reasons to doubt. As I sat and listened to this amazing song, I was whisked back to childhood, and again believed the message in these words. It was a message I had forgotten, and a truth I needed to hear more than I realized. As a person with Parkinson's, it was something I once again needed to believe, and it is something each person battling chronic illness needs to see and feel again. You are special, and you are loved, just the way you are.

Sometimes, this is the greatest gift those surrounding a person with chronic illness can give. People in this daily struggle need to be reminded that even with their difficulties, they are unique, and they are liked. This is a message that often is lost in the pain, and one that needs to be repeated frequently. Sometimes we think our gifts need to be big, but in reality, at times, the smallest kindness means the most and touches a person in a way they never expected. I have been blessed to be surrounded by people who daily remind me of this, and give me this gift each day.

If each of us were truly honest, this is something we all need and something we each need to believe about ourselves. It is something we need to share with those around us as often as we can. Do you struggle to believe this? What in your life makes you feel unlovable and unacceptable? Remember, you were created special, and no matter what your struggles and challenges, you have a unique purpose, and there are many in your life that like you just the way you are. As Mr. Rogers once sang to little Jeffrey, and as he would sing to each of us if given a chance, "I hope that you'll remember, even when you're feeling blue, that it's you... I... like."

CHAPTER 54
HE IS GOOD, NO MATTER WHAT

"He is good". I have heard this song dozens of times. Every year our preschool children, as part of graduation, share this song as a simple reminder that our Lord is good. This year, though, I am having a hard time seeing and believing this. I sit there, listening to this song, and in my head, I think this, but right now, my heart cannot see it.

The last 3 years have been so hard for my family and for me. My health has been in a steady state of decline, to the point that last spring, I had to contemplate early retirement because I could not keep up with everything. We were bouncing from doctor to doctor searching for answers, and now, we were facing, quite possibly, a life-changing diagnosis.

I sat there – shaking, exhausted, in pain, and ready to give up – listening to these precious little ones sing of God's goodness. In my heart and mind, I could not reconcile this idea to my present condition. How could a good God allow this suffering to continue – not just in me, but in others?

Hadn't I already suffered enough? Didn't I have enough challenges? If you really are good, why haven't you given me relief? Why do you keep piling more things on me? My pity party was now full-blown, and I was feeling quite justified in my questions.

As the song continued to play, it got to the bridge, and these precious little ones started thanking God:

Lord, thank you for my parents...
Thank you for my sisters, Lord...
Thank you for answering my prayers...
Thank you for my friends...
Thank you for my home...
Thank you for my goldfish...
Thank you for my church...
Thank you for dying on the cross, Jesus...
Thank you that even when things look bad, You are good.
- Paraphrased from He Is Good, by Steve Green

That last line struck me right between the eyes. "Even when things look bad, You are good." At that moment, God reminded me that yes, things did look bad, but He was with me, and He was good. Through that simple song, I was reminded of a truth I was starting to forget.

You see, I was tying God's goodness to how things were going for me at that moment. I was looking at the struggles, and all that wasn't very good. Instead of continuing to see His goodness, I saw only pain and suffering. In a previous chapter, I shared the statement, "Pain is the great confuser", and that truth was being lived out in me at that moment.

God's goodness is not tied to how I am doing. He is good because He is God. In that simple song, these children were reminding us that we have blessings, and so much to be thankful for. Also, in one sentence, we are told us that even in dark times, He is still good, because His goodness is not based on our circumstances. In spite of trials, we are blessed. Psalm 107:1 says, "Give thanks to the Lord, for He is good, for His steadfast love endures forever." Simply, He is good.

As I left that program, I continued to consider these things, and aside from all my blessing, He was good for another reason. This struggle had brought me closer to Him. Through this trial, I had learned and grown so much, and that also was good. For without this struggle, I might have failed to learn these things.

This little song, and single verse, reminded me of a truth that my pain had begun to obscure. Even though amid my struggle, it was hard to see, He was with me, and He was good. His provisions and strength were with me, and He was helping me see things I had never seen before, and that was indeed good.

This song is a beautiful reminder of the truth, God is good. When you are struggling to see it, finding it impossible to believe, go to His Word, and remember His goodness. Even if in your heart, you do not think so, seek Him and trust that He is. What circumstance is causing you to doubt His goodness? Even when we do not feel it, He is good, and His steadfast love endures forever.

Charles E. Mickles Jr.

Life On This Journey

Do not fear, for I am with you; do not be afraid, for I am your God. I will strengthen you; I will help you; I will hold on to you with My righteous right hand. – Isaiah 41:10

CHAPTER 55
10 THINGS I WISH PEOPLE UNDERSTOOD ABOUT LIVING WITH PARKINSON'S

How do you explain something to a person who has never experienced it? How do they understand what this disease feels like? It is hard for any of us to understand the depth of another's struggle if we have not walked that path ourselves. Still, when we begin to see just a small part of what another is dealing with, it can help us as we work to help them.

I was asked by someone what it was like to have Parkinson's and what I wish others knew and understood about this disease. I thought about it and realized it was harder to describe than I thought. As I began to jot down ideas, I realized how hard it is for even me to wrap my mind around this disease. I ultimately came up with a list of 20 things that I hope I can share with others to help them understand the battle many are facing. Today I will write about the first 10 things that have changed in my life due to this illness:

1. Parkinson's is more than just shaking. So many things are affected that many do not ever see. Anxiety/depression, generalized pain, fatigue, difficulty sleeping, slow

movement, spasms, speech changes, issues swallowing, cognitive problems, and so much more are just part of this "fun" disease. Even when you can't see the "shakes," there is a battle raging in our body.

2. Everyone with Parkinson's is different. How I experience Parkinson's is different than other patients I know. Some symptoms are severe, some do not show up. Some progress slow, while others progress fast — each person struggles differently with this disease, and no two of us are alike.
3. Parkinson's is always there. I never get a break. There are dozens of constant reminders each moment that I have this disease, and there is nothing I can do to change it. There is never a time I forget about having this.
4. Even good days are not good, because there is so much you can't see. Even on days when I am doing "good," everything is still a struggle and takes more effort. Very few things are simple, and most situations require extra effort — even the simple tasks. Even when I am feeling pretty good, there is pain, tremors, stiffness, or any number of other symptoms.
5. There is always constant pain. There is never a time when I am pain-free. I might have less pain that day, but there is still the "white noise" of constant pain in my body. In fact, I cannot remember what a day without pain feels like.
6. I am never getting better, and there is no cure. Unfortunately, at this time, there is no miracle cure. All we can do is slow it down with exercise and control the symptoms with medicines. I can manage the disease and help my body become stronger to fight it, but at this point, I will never get better, and most likely, I will get worse –, and that is a hard thought to deal with.
7. Sometimes I can do stuff, and sometimes I can't. This can change moment by moment. Each moment, I never know who is going to show up — the man who can do stuff, or the man who cannot. I never know which it will be, or which plans or activities I can keep. If you are frustrated by this, imagine how I feel. The uncertainty can drive me nuts some days.
8. It's not just like...(fill in the blank). So often, when people seek to identify with someone, they can minimize that person's struggle. My Parkinson's is not like a cold, or a

person's leg falling asleep, or losing your balance, or being really tired. It is unlike anything I have ever experienced and is not even like any other person's Parkinson's battle.

9. I am not the only one suffering. You see, I have a family – a wife, kids, sister, parents, and many, many more loved ones. Yes, I may be the poster child because I am fighting this battle, but they are hurting and battling this disease just as much as I am. It is hard, especially for my wife and kids, because just like me, they do not get a break, and must watch me suffer and decline. Just like me, they have to deal with all sorts of emotions.

10. Sometimes, it can be very lonely. Especially battling this disease at 44, my family and I many times feel very alone. We know no one near us, and very few even online battling this disease. Sometimes, you do feel like no one understands, and that can be very isolating.

These are just some of the things that make this disease challenging. Day to day, you never know what you are going to face, which is why we must take this disease one day at a time. Fighting this disease is hard, but it helps to have people around us who work to understand our struggle and help us along the way. I am thankful to have many of these people in my life.

CHAPTER 56
10 MORE THINGS I WISH OTHER PEOPLE UNDERSTOOD ABOUT LIVING WITH PARKINSON'S

While the previous chapter (part 1) dealt mostly with the physical aspects of the struggle with this disease, that is just a part of this battle. So much of the struggle I face with Parkinson's Disease is the battle I face in my mind and emotions. In some ways, this part of the disease can be even more of a challenge and makes dealing with the physical struggle that much more difficult. As I considered this aspect of the disease, and how to help others understand, these 10 things stood out to me:

1. There is grief, more than I even realized, and sometimes, I just need to cry. In many ways, I am in mourning. I am mourning the life I thought I would have. I am mourning the death of dreams for myself and for my family. I am mourning the things I can no longer do, and this grief is very real and something I continually feel as this disease progresses.

2. There is self-doubt. Once, so sure of myself, but now, I can't trust my own body from day to day. This causes me to question so many things, from abilities to relationships. It is like continually trying to find your balance and never knowing when the rug will be pulled out from under you. There is always a little voice in my head now questioning everything, and the doubt it causes can be enormous.
3. There are days when I, and even my family, don't want to talk. Sometimes I get tired of hearing myself discuss and explain things. I don't want to give another update, and I am just tired of thinking about it. It is nothing personal. I am not shutting you out. I just don't want to discuss it and deal with it at that moment. I still appreciate you and want your help, so please don't take it personally. Often, there is just really nothing you or I can say to make this better.
4. Sometimes I need to laugh. This disease can be overwhelming and discouraging in so many ways. Personally, I hate being sad, but I love to laugh, so please laugh with me. I will make fun of my condition or tell a joke about it, and if I do, it's okay to laugh with me. Also, if you are able, make me laugh – honestly, I can probably use it.
5. Sometimes it is hard to control myself. Whether it is my body shaking or my emotions, somedays, it is hard to regulate this. My feelings will be up and down, sometimes I will overreact, sometimes I will shake worse than other times. Trust me, I am trying, but please be patient when my reactions, emotions, or body are not cooperating.
6. There are days I am depressed and angry, and I just want to give up. These days, it is hard to see a bright spot. All I can see is that "bad stuff," and on those days, there is no silver lining. When I reach this point, I want to give up and throw in the towel. On those days, please realize I have not given up, but I am just very tired of fighting, and I am feeling discouraged.
7. Sometimes I need a kick in the pants. At times when I am discouraged, I always need understanding, but some days, I just need a kick in the pants to keep moving and fighting

this disease. I need to be reminded of why I am fighting. I need that push to get back up, leave my pity party, and, once again, keep fighting.

8. Most days, I don't know how to deal with me, so I can only imagine how hard it is for you. My wife once told me, "I do not know who I am coming home to?" Guess what, sometimes I do not know either, and that can be very frustrating for us all. My reactions are not always what even I expect them to be and can be all over the place. Just be patient, I promise, I'm not trying to be a punk.

9. There is so much uncertainty, and I am terrified of the future. I told a friend recently, "I am not afraid of dying, because as a believer, I have faith and know where I am going. Honestly, I am terrified of living, and just what that life will look like." Uncertainty of the future and this disease many days is very frightening.

10. Sometimes I just need a hug and someone to sit with me. Many think that there must be some great act of kindness or tremendous gift or service, but sometimes the smallest things mean the most. Many days, I just need someone to put their arm around me, hug me, maybe even cry with me, and just say, "This sucks, but I am here for you." This small and simple gift is the greatest thing anyone can do for those of us and our families caught in this battle.

I have no idea what the future will hold, and I have no idea how difficult things will get. But walking this path with people who care and seek to understand makes this journey that much more easy to travel. Without you helping us, we would not make it, so even when you don't think I am thankful, please know that I am and that your love and care give me the strength to keep fighting and take that next step.

CHAPTER 57
THINGS ONLY A CARE GIVER UNDERSTANDS

"Caregivers go through more than they will ever tell you. They give up a lot and rarely have a social life. They can get sick and emotionally worn out. It is a lot for one person, and you will never know until you have walked the road of a caregiver." - Unknown

My wife described it this way, "Every day it is with us. Chronic Illness has become a part of our lives and seeks to encompass everything. There is no rest, no break, and often, no relief. No matter what I do, I cannot stop the progression, and in many ways, I am helpless to stop the march of this relentless disease, and I am not even the one who has it. As a caregiver, all I can do is watch and support from the shadows."

Caregivers are the forgotten part of Chronic Illness. These beautiful saints fight this battle from the shadows alongside those they love who are suffering. For many, this is a spouse, sibling, child, or friend. Helpless to stop the disease, they strive to provide support and comfort, and many times, they are the forgot part of this Illness.

These angels are the ones that nobody sees. Many times, their part and role, are forgotten. People check on the "patient" all the time, but who checks on them? They take care of their loved one, but many times, no one is there to take care of them. They fight a silent battle of exhaustion, loneliness, and many times neglect. When people ask how things are going, they are asking not about the caregiver, but about the one who is sick. Overshadowed by the one who is ill, they sacrifice their health, rest, dreams, and life for this person – all without being noticed.

For me, that person is my wife. I could not ask for a better wife and caregiver. In our 25 years together, she has watched me go from one medical struggle to another. Many times, she is in the shadows. Being the one with Chronic Illness means people are constantly checking on me and encouraging me – I am the face of this disease for our family. Yet, I am not the only one battling and struggling with this latest challenge.

In a later chapter, I will talk about my children, but today, I want to focus on my wife. She may be the strongest woman I know. She has battled alongside me through so much, and she has never quit. She has strengthened and encouraged me in my lowest points, and she has rejoiced with me at each victory.

When we received this diagnosis, it hit her as hard as it did me, but in a different way. Once again, she was placed on the sidelines, forced to watch her partner fight a losing battle. Yes, I was the one who was sick, but she was the one forced to watch her husband struggle and decline, helpless to stop it. She was there to pick up the pieces and be my strength when I had none, and she was the one that had to deal with the loss this disease created.

As we sat and talked one night, I asked her to describe some things she and others felt as caregivers. I wanted a window into what she, my helper on this journey, faced each and every day. Some of what she shared surprised me, and some of the things she shared as struggles I had not even considered. I realized that so often, I was focused on my battle, just as others were, and totally missed the silent battle she was waging.

Mine's Parkinson's, What's Yours?

As we spoke, she shared how hard it was to watch the one you love suffer, and the utter feeling of helplessness to do anything about it. This disease did not just take an emotional toll on me, but on her as well. She, like me, was experiencing sadness and grief. She was hurting because I was hurting. As she watched me decline, she was helpless to stop it, yet even in this helplessness, determination to fight on was bred.

We also talked about how people don't always understand. It is not like the flu, or a passing cold, or being stiff and sore in the morning. It is a nonstop, never-ending drumbeat that follows us. Even on good days, it is there, and there is still pain and sorrow. There is no rest, and there is never a "break" from dealing with this. Just because she is not sick, does not mean she is not in a deep battle herself.

Because of this, especially for a young family, battling an "old persons" disease is very isolating. We can't do the things that healthy families do. It is something we always have to consider when doing any activity. In our age group, there is no one near us battling this disease, and finding support, that genuinely understands, can be very hard. Alone, she is facing battles she should not have to suffer for another 25-30 years, and there is no one in our station of life to say, "I get it."

We are forced to make decisions that no young couple should, and planning for the future is almost a joke. Since we have no way of knowing the course this Illness will take, we get to have fun adventures like meeting with Elder Care Lawyers. Not only this, but the financial burden placed on families in this situation due to medical bills and care is extensive, further cutting into the things our family can do.

Sadly, she also takes the brunt of my hurt, frustrations, and anger. She sees me at my worse, when I am ready to give up, because I am done fighting. She deals with the angry over-reactions and outbursts that others do not see and the mood swings that occur in this day-by-day fight. When I have no one else to explode to, she is there, and takes it, and loves me through it. Because I am hurting, sometimes, I hurt her, even when in my heart I don't want to. In spite of the hurt I cause her, she loves and supports me.

Often, these beautiful people, who are the true, forgotten heroes of this disease, stand in the shadows, supporting those they love. They are overlooked and not seen for all they do to try to make this a manageable fight. While I am suffering from Parkinson's, she is suffering from its effects on me and continues to stand with me through the worst.

Caregivers are special people. They give in secret, with no fanfare, when all others are gone. They never stop, never have a break, and many times, are never recognized or encouraged. They hold us up and support us, and take the brunt of our hurt, exhaustion, and anger. Like us, they never get a rest, and in some ways, fight a much harder battle. They are the true heroes in this fight as they give up their lives, their dreams, their desires to help care for another.

I am continually humbled by the love and support my wife gives me as I battle this awful disease. She strengthens me to fight each day, and her love and sacrifice, I can never repay. I love her and am more thankful for her than she will ever know. She is the true warrior and hero in this fight.

As you minister to those in the battle, don't forget those in the shadows supporting them. They need encouragement and love, just as we do. They need someone to check on them and see how they are doing. They need others to support and strengthen them. Maybe it is a note, a prayer, a dinner out, or a fun excursion. Perhaps it is a hug, a shoulder to cry on, or an ear to listen.

Just like those of us who are sick, they need all of these things, and so much more. Without them, we would never be able to keep fighting. Thank you, Kimberly, for fighting beside me, and thank you to all the caregivers who give so much every single day. We could not do this without you, and we are more thankful for you than you will ever know.

CHAPTER 58
WHAT'S IT LIKE FOR KIDS WALKING THIS PATH

Dealing with hard situations as an adult is hard enough. Many times we do not know how to respond or how to cope. Our emotions get the best of us, and we fight these circular battles in our mind that will not stop. Even with all of this, though, we are good at wearing masks and pretending all is well. For children, that is a different story entirely.

Kids, in some ways, let it all hang out. Usually, it is easy to read their moods and feelings. You can tell when they are overwhelmed, and when something is bothering them. They are not quite the actors we as adults are, and not as practiced at wearing that mask.

Yet, at times, life steps in and changes that. Because of hardship, either personally or with a close family member, they are forced to grow up more quickly. Before they should, they must learn coping strategies, and are forced to walk through many challenging days. They, too, learn to put up the mask, and pretend all is well, and no one around them realizes just how they are struggling.

Mine's Parkinson's, What's Yours?

I have two children, and there are many days when I am just not sure how they are doing. They have learned to put up a mask and pretend all is good because they do not want to add to my burden. They dismiss what they are feeling, and hide how they are hurting, all in the name of being strong for me, and not laying an even more significant burden on my back.

Sometimes, it's too much for them, and they seek escape. It can be out of the house with friends or inside the home with things they enjoy. Whatever the form, it is so they do not have to think about it. They, just like me, get tired of the day-to-day battle, and sometimes just want to forget and not think about it.

They miss out on things other children and families can do, because of the limits my body places on me. Sometimes, for some activities, they must have a "stand-in" dad, because I simply cannot do it. Year after year, they miss out on some events, trips, and experiences, because that money was used to maintain this broken body.

It can be a lot for anyone, let alone a child, to take in. As I prepared this chapter, I spoke with my children. I wanted to hear where they really were with this, and what they struggled with. I wanted them to open up about their struggle, and part of that came with an opportunity to share our story with students at our school.

While this was challenging, it was beneficial and healing and forced us to have some discussions we might not have had otherwise. It was hard listening to them, because I knew there was nothing I could do to ease their pain, and I knew that their pain was because of me. In many ways, it was good talking with them, because it brought us together and helped us walk together through this latest struggle.

So I asked my kids to tell me what it is like having a father with Parkinson's? What is hard? What is unexpected? As a teenager, how are they processing it? I got a lot of answers I had not even thought of, and it helped give me a window into their struggle. In some ways, they were struggling like me, in other ways, it was totally different.

Just like for me, the future is terrifying. There is sadness and pain, and it isn't very comforting to think of the possibilities of the future. Because of how scary the future is, it is easy to be overwhelmed and to try to avoid it or suppress feelings, so they do not overtake us. Just like me, they never get a break, and in some ways, it is always on their mind.

This can lead to feelings of frustration. It is easy to look at this and see the unfairness of it all. This frustration and feelings of unfairness are accentuated by the things my children must miss out on. Whether it is merely fun activities or events, or even big vacations due to the financial burden of these diseases. Sometimes the struggle to "Just do it" means my children miss out on experiences.

It is also hard sometimes for them when I "blow-up" at things. When my frustration comes through and spills out on to them. They experience the hurt my anger and frustration causes, and I make it harder for them to cope. There is also much isolation in this struggle, because how many children have parents battling things like this at their age?

Negative emotions aren't the only thing we deal with. We have also found a lot of humor and many things to laugh about. One benefit has been a whole new selection of Dad Jokes. And yes, my daughter rolls her eyes. They are learning in this process that it is still okay to laugh. When we take time to joke and laugh, the future does not seem quite so scary.

Just like me, they are learning to take it one day at a time while processing their emotions. In the end, I know it will make them stronger, but it is still hard to watch. I do not know that any of us will ever be okay with my diagnosis. Still, hopefully, I can help them as they help me on this journey – a journey that none of us wanted to take.

CHAPTER 59
HOW DOES THIS AFFECT FAMILIES

Every family is different, and every family is faced with struggles. We all battle problems, sickness, financial struggles, and on and on the list could go. When you are diagnosed with a chronic illness, everything for a family changes. With this struggle, every area is affected, and nothing is left untouched.

Battling arthritis was bad enough. Having three hip replacements was more than enough. These things already limited my family and me in so many ways. Developing Parkinson's Disease almost pushed us over the edge. Before we had a diagnosis and treatment had started, I was beginning to declining physically. In those months, we began to realize just how challenging this fight would end up being.

When we heard my diagnosis, we knew our lives forever would be changed. From this moment on, there was no break, no reprieve; it would always be here. We knew there would be constant adjustments to our lives due to my changing health, and nothing would quite be the same.

We had already seen how it would limit our activities, and how tiring some days would be mentally, physically, and emotionally. We often experienced the financial toll my health took with over $150,000 spent over the years maintaining me (I know, I am a pricey little thing).

Each day and year, there were new things to mourn and grieve. We dealt with a whole host of emotions including sadness, frustration, anger, doubt, fear, laughter, and anything else you can think of. Through it all, we worked to protect one another's feelings and not lay an even more substantial burden on each other.

Yet, as we walk this path, I have been surprised to see that we have not just experienced adverse effects from this disease. I honestly have been surprised at some of the positive effects. While sometimes it did drive us apart, as we found our footing, instead of destroying us, it strengthened us as a family.

It helped bind us together and, in many ways, hold each other tighter. Some days, we just held each other and cried, while other days, we just could not stop laughing. We spent time talking and sharing our innermost fears and doubts while celebrating the blessings we had.

We saw things differently than we had before and began to see what really was essential. This disease bound us together in unexpected ways and showed us the importance of the time we had. We realized how much we honestly had to be thankful for.

While I would not choose this path, I am thankful for the family I have with me and love and support we have for one another. I am blessed that as hard as this road is, it has forced us together, and not driven us apart. In every circumstance, this is the choice we are faced with. Will it strengthen us and cement us together, or will it destroy us and be the wedge that pulls us apart? Adversity can have both effects, and we choose which it will be.

Mine's Parkinson's, What's Yours?

What in your life is difficult? How has it affected you and your relationships? Remember, you choose, so choose wisely. Allow the struggle to bind you together deeply as you love, strengthen, and support one another. Don't choose to walk this path alone – find your tribe, and allow the struggle to bind you together.

CHAPTER 60
REFLECTION – WHAT A DIFFERENCE A YEAR MAKES

Christmas, 2018. My latest round of tests had just been completed. Once again, I had heard the phrase that I hated to hear, "Everything looks good; nothing seems wrong." Again and again, I heard that I was fine, yet my body was screaming something else. In pain, exhausted, and struggling to hang on, I was at my limit, and I could not keep going. It was a very dark place.

A little over a year ago, I sent a message to my most trusted doctors, one of which had been helping me since the age of 15. "Good morning Dr. M. and Dr. B. I am writing you because I really don't know what to do at this point. Things are getting worse, and we don't seem to have any answers...I'm losing the ability to do things, such as writing, typing, and grasping objects. My strength is frail, and I'm having a lot of numbness and pain. I've been to a hand and wrist specialist...I've had a brain and spine MRI, and they keep finding NOTHING. Everything that can be scanned has, and still no results. My tremors are getting worse, and there just does not seem to be answers. What should be my next steps, are there things we need to look at or am I just losing my mind. I'm just not sure what to do, and I desperately need some answers and help."

Mine's Parkinson's, What's Yours?

I thought I was losing it. I kept hearing nothing is wrong, and everything in my body was SCREAMING the opposite. I was discouraged, depressed, and ready to give up. People were watching me struggle and deteriorate and were helpless to do anything. I remember telling my wife, "I don't think I can keep doing this; I am not sure I can go on."

Scared, hurting, discouraged, I did not know where to turn and what to do. Darkness was enveloping and overwhelming me. Now a year later, I am learning just how bad I looked. I have had people tell me, "I thought you were dying; you looked like you were 80 years old; you looked awful; you looked so discouraged and in so much pain." (I know, encouraging) And the reality was, they were right, and I was feeling the same way. Little did I know at that time what was awaiting my family and me.

All of this translated into hopelessness. After years of searching, still no answers were apparent. With no idea what we were even fighting, it was hard to know how to proceed. Not knowing was an almost unbearable weight for the family and for me.

Six months later, we finally had answers – just not the ones we wanted, but at least we knew what we were facing. Even with the answers, there was still much uncertainty about our future. At least, though, we knew what we were dealing with. As we began down the Parkinson's Road, I must admit, it was not smooth sailing. There were bumps and potholes and roadblocks along the way.

As we have walked this path, God has already shown us many things; some of which are in this book. We have educated ourselves, made difficult decisions, and tried to process all the emotions and physical challenges that we now face. Each day brings new challenges, and while there are many good days, there are also many dark ones as well. But things definitely look better than they did 12 months ago.

The change has been more than physical. With medication and exercise (which I hate), my body is stronger, and I can once again function almost normally. There are still struggles, but overall, I am feeling much better. While this has been good and exciting, for me, that has only been part of this year's change.

Last year, I was ready to give up. Exhausted, in constant pain, with no answers, I did not think I could go on. I was discouraged, angry, depressed, and hopeless that anything would change or get better. No one had answers, and I just kept getting worse. I was isolating myself from others. I was struggling as a father and husband and letting my physical condition drive us apart.

As I consider this year, and where I was a year ago, I realize that my physical pain and struggle was not the most significant battle I was facing. My spirit was crushed, and I really had no hope. I was ready to give up. Yes, finding answers helped, but in reality, sometime in the future, the treatments will stop working. I will once again struggle significantly physically. When that day comes, how will I choose to respond?

This last year, more than anything, I realized that life without hope is unbearable. As hard as it was dealing with my physical challenges, not having faith was even harder. I was left with the decision, whether I had answers or not, whether I knew what was wrong or not, would I trust Him? Would I rest in the hope He could provide? Would I rest in the peace that He is in control? Would I allow Him to be my portion and my provision?

I realize that my answers to these questions are much more important than my physical state. The attitude and beliefs I choose to face these challenges with is often more critical than the struggles themselves. As I look back over this last year, I am doing better physically, mentally, and spiritually. More days than not, I am seeking to rest in Him and His plan for me. It is not always easy, but instead of giving up without hope, I am fighting with Him as my hope. All I can say is, "What a difference a year makes."

THE FIVE (MOST IMPORTANT LESSONS I HAVE LEARNED SO FAR ON THIS JOURNEY)

Written January, 2020

It has been a little over 6 months since I first heard those words, "You have Parkinson's Disease." Four small words that turned our family's world upside down. Since that proclamation, it has felt like drinking from a fire hydrant. Medications to research, side effects to manage, elder care planning meetings, education about the disease, and on and on and on it goes. So much to learn; so many things to consider.

As I have shared in other chapters, some days, it was very overwhelming and scary. Sometimes we laughed, and many times we cried, but through it all, God began working in our little family and helped us as we took our first steps into the unknown. Some days were easier than others, but every day we knew He was with us.

As I look back over the last 6 months, so many things have changed, and so many things stand out to me. Of all the lessons I have begun to learn, these 5 have been the most impactful:

Charles E. Mickles Jr.

1. Will I trust Him? In those days after diagnosis, this is one of the first questions God asked me over and over again. In the face of devastating news, and a very uncertain future, would I trust Him? I will be honest, sometimes the answer I gave Him was "No" because all I could see was the pain and suffering. Yet even in these times of doubt, He loved me and showed Himself faithful. Even though some days it is hard, yes, I can trust Him.

2. It is okay to grieve. In life, there is sorrow, and some days are very hard, no matter who you are. In the weeks following my news, there were many tears, and sometimes there still are. I was grieving for my situation, my future, my family, and so many other things. Grieving is necessary. It does not mean I am not trusting God. It simply means that this is hard, and I am hurting, and that is okay. Grieving, very often, is a necessary step in healing, accepting, and moving forward. Sometimes, tears are needed.

3. I need to cherish every moment. When I heard those words, one of the first questions that popped into my mind was, "How long do I have?" The answer (as it was before my diagnosis) was, "who knows." But coming face to face with this illness made me realize how many times I was not intentional, and how often I failed to make the most of and cherish every moment. I have realized how special each moment is and how they will never come again. Living in each moment, and cherishing every memory is a must in life.

4. Sometimes, you just need to laugh. So many times over these past two months, I have really needed to laugh. The weight of this latest problem and all that came with it was overwhelming, and it was very easy to let sorrow take over. Yet in those moments, I was reminded time and again that "a merry heart is a good medicine..." I saw that laughter and joy were needed on this walk, now more than ever. Sometimes, I just had to stop and laugh.

5. No matter what, I can choose hope. I have realized that I choose how I will look at life and my future. I can decide whether or not I will live in despair or look with hope to the one who holds my future.

Even though there are days when hope seems very dim, it is still there, and I can choose to look to that or focus on the problems before me. Hope depends on faith, and faith is simply a trust in what we cannot see. No matter how hard the struggle, our hope is in Him and Him alone.

There are so many things God is continuing to show me. Some lessons are just refreshers, others are deep and hard, but through these lessons, I am learning to trust Him more deeply. I know that whatever comes my way, He is with me. There will be times of grief and times of laughter, and each of these moments, I will cherish as special, for they will not come again. Can I trust Him? Yes, I can put my trust in Him because in Him, I have hope.

A FINAL THOUGHT: EVEN WHEN...

As years go, this has been one of the hardest. I am definitely not sad to bid farewell to 2019 (although 2020 is beginning to just look like part 2, the sequel). It has not only been my personal struggles but so many difficulties of people I love surrounding me. So many events and challenges that have left me asking God, "Really? We need another issue to deal with?" It has seemed like burden after burden, sorrow after sorrow have been laid on the shoulders of my family and others that I love.

This year, I have come face to face with a body that was failing, and in a sense, my own mortality. I have had to accept that my body was broken, there was no cure, and all we could do was try to slow things down. I have felt alone and worthless. I have had my faith shaken (as my body was literally trembling). I have had to accept the reality that short of a miracle, I will not get better, and over time, will only get worse.

This year, a pastor friend and I were talking, and he started using the phrase, "Even when...", speaking about God. As he spoke with me, he reminded me that even when we are struggling, we can still trust God. Over these past 6 months, I have come face to face with many

"Even when" moments. As the year has progressed, I began writing down some of the "Even when moments" I was walking through.

I am learning that even when I don't, He does, and He will provide:

Even when I'm in pain…I will trust that He is the Great Physician and will give me strength.
Even when I'm tired of fighting…God will strengthen me to keep fighting if I allow Him to.
Even when my body is failing…His grace will be sufficient, and His power will be made perfect in my weakness.
Even when our finances are tight…He is Jehovah Jireh, our provider.
Even when we do not understand…He does, and he knows what to do.
Even when I am facing an uncertain future…He knows the plans He has for my life.
Even when my mind is failing…He will not forget me or His promises.
Even when we are overwhelmed with stress…He will provide peace and rest.
Even when I have no answers…He knows everything, and His answers are the best.
Even when I am overwhelmed…He will carry me and hold me.
Even when I am alone…He is still there, walking beside me.
Even when I can't go any further…He will help me take that next step.
Even when everything seems to be falling apart…He holds everything in His hands.
Even when God seems silent…He is still speaking to me through His Word and other believers.
Even when I am discouraged…He will encourage me and give me the courage I need.
Even when my heart is broken…He will heal and mend that broken heart.
Even when I am ready to give up…He will be there to support me and help me keep going.

Charles E. Mickles Jr.

Even when I am sad and discouraged...He will be my source of joy.
Even when I can find no rest or peace...He will provide both.
Even when I am afraid...He will be my rock and fortress, my deliverer, and in Him, can I trust.

"Even when" changes the entire story, and provides hope, where there is hopelessness. It reminds us that His strength is perfect, and He will give us daily what we need to do His will. The only catch is, we must let Him. We must allow Him to change our temporal viewpoint to an eternal one. If we allow Him to do this, it really does change everything. When we see things from His perspective, we can have hope, for He will never leave us or forsake us, because His strength is perfect, and His love is never-ending. When we find ourselves in struggles and difficulties, we must remember that even when we are facing something, when God is involved, it changes everything. Even when I do not know how this disease will affect my family and me, God does, and His power, strength, love, and peace will sustain us.

Whatever you are facing, whatever you are struggling through, never forget that He is with you, He will strengthen you, and He will never leave you or forsake you. As you walk this path of life, remember this. It does not mean your life will be trouble-free, but it does mean you have someone with you through it all, even when it seems everything is wrong.

We all have difficulties to walk through and we choose daily how to face each challenge. What challenge are you facing and how will you choose to face it? "Even when" you are walking through difficulties, remember, He is with you. My battle is Parkinson's Disease, what's yours?

WHAT READERS ARE SAYING...

And there you have it! Thanks for taking the time to put this battle into words. At 78 years old I can be grateful to reach my 70's before my battle begun. I so admire your stamina and courage and pray that you will reap the reward of greater comfort and cure soon. Stay strong. — Anonymous

Not a club anyone would choose to belong to, but nonetheless they walk the journey. Thank you for your transparency. This will be life for others. ♥#courageous — Lisa

Real. Encouraging. Faithful. — Pam

It is heart-felt journey that can help you walk through the tough times. It is such an encouragement. — Kimberly

What a description!! It's my life in someone else's words. Well done for digging deep and giving an honest look at "our" life. — Anonymous

Thank you for making me think through the hope we have with eternal thinking. God allows these things for a reason and He always wants what is good!! — Joyce

It is a real and a honest documentation of a great man's journey. — Steger

Your words help to give us encouragement no matter what we are going through. I think sometimes I feel if I tell God ok I am at the end of my rope then he will immediately take over a fix the situation. That is not promised. What is, is that he is with us during our adversities. — Anonymous

Thank you for being transparent. — Frances

Hey Friend, this is a great blog entry. Thanks for sharing and inviting us on your journey. It is a pleasure to get to walk with you thru this season. — Mike

It is as if you looked into my life and wrote down my thoughts. Many do not know what my daily battles are like. This would be an excellent representation.
— *Kim*

It provides an ongoing picture of a disease that can be devastating as it begins to invade the body, lifestyle, and family life, and ways he and his family face daily and new challenges. Some or all may offer a light to the darkness that Parkinson's can bring. This family was my neighbor for 16+ years. They are genuine!!! Ched truly hopes to help others by writing his journey. — *Sharon*

This is real life. My life with Parkinson's disease. As if my heart is being examined and the words of my life are put to the page. — *Kim*

My life explained. — *Lisa*

ACKNOWLEDGEMENTS

It would be impossible to thank all of the people who have made an impact on my life. There have been so many who the Lord has used to help me, and for each of you I am truly thankful. There are a few, though, who have been especially supportive as I have written this book, and throughout my life, who I would like to thank.

I want to say a special thank you to my wife, Kimberly. I am so thankful that the Lord put us together. You have been with me through my greatest joys and some of my darkest hours. You believed in me and this book before anyone else, and you were the one who first challenged me to write these things down. You have encouraged, supported, and helped me along the way, and been my strength when I had none. For this, and whatever the future holds, I am deeply thankful.

I wish to thank my children, Alyssa and RJ. You are a great source of joy and both of you are very precious to me. I am blessed to be your father. You are both wonderful testimonies of Christ, and I am daily impressed by the grace, strength, and peace I see in you as we walk this new path as a family. To all my adopted children and students – you know who you are – love you and I am so proud of who you are becoming, and I am thankful to be part of your life. Special thanks to my "sons" – Elijah, Nate, Paul, and Greg – I love each of you!

Thank you to all of our family. Through our lives, both my wife and I have had very supportive families that have helped us in every way imaginable. I owe a special thank you to our parents: Charlie, Pam, Richard, and Bonnie for standing by us. You helped make us what we are today. You have loved us, cared for us, and blessed us in ways that you will never know. Also, a special thanks to my little sisters, Karen and Kimberly; I love you. Your lives have been such a testimony to me. Thanks for putting up with me all these years. Also, my brothers and sisters-in-law Adam, Rick, Nikki, Jenn, and David – thank you for your support and love during this battle. To all of our extended family – your impact and love continue to give me strength as I walk this path.

My family and I wish to thank our church body at Lifepoint for caring for us during this time and welcoming us as we began this new chapter.

Lighthouse Christian School and Fellowship, and my family of staff, parents, and student – I love you all. Teachers (especially the elementary teachers and Kate) and staff – I could not do this without you and you are each family to me – thank you just is not enough. You have been a special part of my life for over 30 years and have been with my family through thick and thin. Thank you for walking beside us.

To "the guys (Gerald, Scott, and Jeff)," thanks for your friendship over the last 30+ years. You are the friends of my youth, really, my brothers, and have walked with me for my entire "health journey" – thank you for helping me in more ways than you will ever know.

To my other brothers – Bill, Kevin, "D", Mark, Jason, Ben, Kevin, Steve, and so many others – thank you for your love, encouragement, and just being there when I need you.

A special thank you for my editors and promotion team – Jody, Pam (mom), Bonnie, Adam, Savannah, and Greg – thank you for helping to make this work better, and for investing you time into my dream.

To all the multitude of people who continue to support and love us – you know who you are – thank you. We are daily blessed by you. There are many whom I wish I could thank personally, and I could fill a book just with that. So many who have blessed us and cared for us when we needed it most, and who truly were the hands and feet of Christ. So many people have touched my life and my family in a way that they will never know. To each of you, thank you for helping me and blessing my family along the way. Know that you have made a lasting impact and a difference.

REFERENCES/SOURCE MATERIALS

Our Journey Begins
1. Jeremiah 29:11, *The Holy Bible, English Standard Version (ESV).* (2007). Wheaton, Ill.: Crossway Bibles.

Chapter 1
1. Psalm 27:13-14, *The Holy Bible, New American Standard (NASB).* (1971). LaHabra, CA: Foundation Publications, for the Lockman Foundation.

Chapter 2
1. Psalm 22:2, *The Holy Bible, English Standard Version (ESV).* (2007). Wheaton, Ill.: Crossway Bibles.

Chapter 3
1. Matthew 6:34, *The Holy Bible, King James Version (KJV),* 1611.
2. II Corinthians 12:9, *The Holy Bible, King James Version (KJV),* 1611.

Chapter 5
1. I Thessalonians 5:18, *The Holy Bible, King James Version (KJV),* 1611.
2. Philippians 4:4, *The Holy Bible, King James Version (KJV),* 1611.
3. Nehemiah 8:10, *The Holy Bible, English Standard Version (ESV).* (2007). Wheaton, Ill.: Crossway Bibles.
4. Philippians 4:6, *The Holy Bible, English Standard Version (ESV).* (2007). Wheaton, Ill.: Crossway Bibles.
5. Proverbs 3:5, *The Holy Bible, English Standard Version (ESV).* (2007). Wheaton, Ill.: Crossway Bibles.
6. Ecclesiastes 3:4, *The Holy Bible, English Standard Version (ESV).* (2007). Wheaton, Ill.: Crossway Bibles.
7. Psalm 34:18, *The Holy Bible, New International Version (NIV).* (1984). Grand Rapids: Zondervan Publishing House.
8. Psalm 147:3, *The Holy Bible, English Standard Version (ESV).* (2007). Wheaton, Ill.: Crossway Bibles.

9. *Matthew 5:4, The Holy Bible, English Standard Version (ESV). (2007). Wheaton, Ill.: Crossway Bibles.*
10. *Romans 12:15, The Holy Bible, English Standard Version (ESV). (2007). Wheaton, Ill.: Crossway Bibles.*

Dark Days

1. *Psalm 23:4, The Holy Bible, New International Version (NIV). (1984). Grand Rapids: Zondervan Publishing House.*

Chapter 6

1. *Isaiah 40:29, 31, The Holy Bible, New International Version (NIV). (1984). Grand Rapids: Zondervan Publishing House.*
2. *Psalm 46:1, The Holy Bible, English Standard Version (ESV). (2007). Wheaton, Ill.: Crossway Bibles.*
3. *Nehemiah 8:10, The Holy Bible, English Standard Version (ESV). (2007). Wheaton, Ill.: Crossway Bibles.*
4. *Psalm 28:7, The Holy Bible, English Standard Version (ESV). (2007). Wheaton, Ill.: Crossway Bibles.*
5. *Psalm 118:14, The Holy Bible, New International Version (NIV). (1984). Grand Rapids: Zondervan Publishing House.*

Chapter 7

1. *Hebrews 11:1, The Holy Bible, English Standard Version (ESV). (2007). Wheaton, Ill.: Crossway Bibles.*

Chapter 8

1. *Psalm 30:11, The Holy Bible, English Standard Version (ESV). (2007). Wheaton, Ill.: Crossway Bibles.*
2. *Lamentations 3:22-23, The Holy Bible, English Standard Version (ESV). (2007). Wheaton, Ill.: Crossway Bibles.*

Chapter 9

1. *Hebrews 11:1, The Holy Bible, English Standard Version (ESV). (2007). Wheaton, Ill.: Crossway Bibles.*
2. *Psalm 121:1-2, The Holy Bible, English Standard Version (ESV). (2007). Wheaton, Ill.: Crossway Bibles.*

Chapter 10
    1.   Spafford, Horatio. <u>It Is Well With My Soul</u>. 1873.

My Focus
    1.   II Corinthians 4:18, The Holy Bible, King James Version (KJV), 1611.

Chapter 12
    1.   John Milton

Chapter 14
    1.   Psalm 23:4, The Holy Bible, English Standard Version (ESV). (2007). Wheaton, Ill.: Crossway Bibles.

Chapter 16
    1.   Capra, F., Stewart, J., & Liberty Films. (1946). <u>It's A Wonderful Life</u>. Los Angeles, California: Liberty Films.
    2.   Numbers 6:24-26, The Holy Bible, New International Version (NIV). (1984). Grand Rapids: Zondervan Publishing House.

Well, This Stinks
    1.   John 14:27, The Holy Bible, New International Version (NIV). (1984). Grand Rapids: Zondervan Publishing House.

Chapter 17:
    1.   Jeremiah 17:7, The Holy Bible, New International Version (NIV). (1984). Grand Rapids: Zondervan Publishing House.

Letting Go
    1.   Philippians 4:6-7, The Holy Bible, New International Version (NIV). (1984). Grand Rapids: Zondervan Publishing House.

Bright Spots In My Darkness
    1.   Luke 18:1, The Amplified Bible (AMP): Containing the Amplified Old Testament and the Amplified New Testament. Grand Rapids, Michigan: Zondervan Publishing House, 1965.

Learning To Laugh Again
1. Proverbs 22:17, *The Holy Bible, English Standard Version (ESV)*. *(2007)*. *Wheaton, Ill.: Crossway Bibles*.

Chapter 30
1. Proverbs 17:22, *The Holy Bible: The New King James Version*. *1982. Nashville: Thomas Nelson*.

So Many Questions
1. II Corinthians 12:9-10, *The Holy Bible, New International Version (NIV)*. *(1984). Grand Rapids: Zondervan Publishing House*.

Chapter 34
1. Francis of Assisi

Chapter 35:
1. Lois Binstock, *The Power of Faith (Prentice-Hall)* taken from the book: *The Speaker's Book of Illustrative Stories, by Maxwell Droke. Droke House: Indianapolis, Indiana, 1956*.

Emotional Ups and Downs
1. Philippians 4:11-13, *The Holy Bible, New American Standard (NASB). (1971). LaHabra, CA: Foundation Publications, for the Lockman Foundation*.

Chapter 36
1. Romans 12:15, *The Holy Bible, English Standard Version (ESV). (2007). Wheaton, Ill.: Crossway Bibles*.

Chapter 37
1. Dr. Phil Show, Phil McGraw.

Chapter 38
1. Deuteronomy 31:8, *The Holy Bible, New International Version (NIV). (1984). Grand Rapids: Zondervan Publishing House*.
2. Psalm 46:1-2, *The Holy Bible, English Standard Version (ESV). (2007). Wheaton, Ill.: Crossway Bibles*.

3. *Psalm 56:3, The Holy Bible: Holman Christian Standard Version (CSB). 2009. Nashville: Holman Bible Publishers.*

Chapter 39
1. *Psalm 23:4, The Holy Bible, English Standard Version (ESV). (2007). Wheaton, Ill.: Crossway Bibles.*

Walking This Journey Together
1. *Romans 12:5, 10. & 16a, The Holy Bible, English Standard Version (ESV). (2007). Wheaton, Ill.: Crossway Bibles.*

Chapter 41
1. *Psalm 23, The Holy Bible, English Standard Version (ESV). (2007). Wheaton, Ill.: Crossway Bibles.*

Chapter 43:
1. *Deuteronomy 31:6, The Holy Bible, English Standard Version (ESV). (2007). Wheaton, Ill.: Crossway Bibles.*

Chapter 44
1. *Parkinson's Statistics can be found in numerous places including: Parkinson's Foundation, the Michael J. Fox Foundation, and other sources.*

Chapter 47
1. *Marriage vows*

What I Am Learning
1. *Psalm 90:12, The Holy Bible, English Standard Version (ESV). (2007). Wheaton, Ill.: Crossway Bibles.*

Chapter 48
1. *Genesis 50:20, The Holy Bible, New International Version (NIV). (1984). Grand Rapids: Zondervan Publishing House.*
2. *Lamentations 3:21-24, The Holy Bible, New International Version (NIV). (1984). Grand Rapids: Zondervan Publishing House.*

Chapter 50
1. Spafford, Horatio. <u>It Is Well With My Soul</u>. 1873.

Chapter 53
1. It's You I Like, Fred Rogers.

Chapter 54
1. Steve Green, He is Good.
2. Psalm 107:1, The Holy Bible, English Standard Version (ESV). (2007). Wheaton, Ill.: Crossway Bibles.

Life On This Journey
1. Isaiah 41:10, The Holy Bible: Holman Christian Standard Version (CSB). 2009. Nashville: Holman Bible Publishers.

Afterwards
1. II Corinthians 12:7-10, The Holy Bible, English Standard Version (ESV). (2007). Wheaton, Ill.: Crossway Bibles.
2. Proverbs 17:22, The Holy Bible, English Standard Version (ESV). (2007). Wheaton, Ill.: Crossway Bibles.
3. Psalm 27:13-14, The Holy Bible, English Standard Version (ESV). (2007). Wheaton, Ill.: Crossway Bibles.

ABOUT THE AUTHOR

Charles Mickles is a Christian, author, speaker, and an elementary school principal. He has worked with children his entire career, and enjoys helping them as they learn and grow. He is a graduate of Liberty University with a Bachelor's and Master's Degree in Education. He is married with two teenage children, and loves science fiction (Star Wars, Star Trek, Lord of the Rings), music of all kinds, movies, and reading. Charles has battled Chronic Illness since 15 (R. Arthritis), had three hip replacements, and most recently has been diagnosed with Parkinson's Disease, all by the age of 44. He has been featured as a New Channel 5 "Excellent Educator", has received the "Legacy of Leaders" awards, and has been selected as "Teacher of the Year" numerous times. Having served as a Deacon, Elder, Licensed Minister, Bible study leader, and in many additional capacities, he is faithfully involved in his local church. He is the author of the book, <u>Life Through a Father's Eyes</u>, and is currently writing two blogs, and has been published on "Yahoo Lifestyles", "MSN", and "The Mighty" websites. He currently resides outside of Nashville, TN.

https://myjourneywithparkinsonsdaybyday.blogspot.com/

https://lessonsfromagalaxyfarfaraway.blogspot.com/

To schedule a speaking engagement or for other inquiries, please email Charles at chmickles@gmail.com.

Made in the USA
Monee, IL
09 August 2020